MW00988227

A LIFE DISPLACED

A Mennonite Woman's
Flight from War-Torn Poland

Mennonite Reflections
Volume 3

Mennonite Reflections

Mennonite Reflections is a monograph series dedicated to the preservation and publication of materials that explore the Mennonite experience. The series is published through the Institute of Anabaptist Mennonite Studies, Conrad Grebel College, University of Waterloo, in cooperation with Pandora Press.

The Silence Echoes: Memoirs of Trauma and Tears
   Edited and translated by Sarah Dyck, 1997.

Lifting the Veil: Mennonite Life in Russia Before the Revolution
   Jacob H. Janzen. Edited with an introduction by Leonard Friesen. Translated by Walter Klaassen, 1998.

**A Life Displaced: A Mennonite Woman's Flight
   from War-Torn Poland**
   Edna Schroeder Thiessen and Angela Showalter, 2000.

A LIFE DISPLACED

A Mennonite Woman's
Flight from War-Torn Poland

by

Edna Schroeder Thiessen

and

Angela Showalter

Published by
Pandora Press
Copublished with
Herald Press

Canadian Cataloguing in Publication Data

Thiessen, Edna Schroeder, 1926-
  A life displaced : a Mennonite woman's flight from war-torn Poland

(Mennonite reflections, ISSN 1480-3895)
ISBN 0-9685543-2-6

1. Thiessen, Edna Schroeder, 1926- . 2. World War, 1939-1945 – Personal narratives, Polish. 3. World War, 1939-1945 – Refugees – Biography. 4. World War, 1939-1945 – Mennonites – Poland. 5. Women refugees – Poland – Biography. 6. Mennonite Women – Poland – Biography. 7. Women refugees – Canada – Biography. 8. Mennonite women – Canada – Biography. I. Showalter, Angela, 1972- . II. Title. III. Series.

D811.5.T44 1999   940.53'086'91   C99-932735-6

A LIFE DISPLACED:
A MENNONITE WOMAN'S FLIGHT FROM WAR-TORN POLAND

Copyright © 2000 by Pandora Press
51 Pandora Avenue N.
Kitchener, Ontario, N2H 3C1

Co-published with Herald Press,
Scottdale, Pennsylvania/Waterloo, Ontario

International Standard Book Number: **0-9685543-2-6**
Printed in Canada on acid-free paper

Cover design, graphics, and map by Jan Gleysteen

08 07 06 05 04 03 02 01 00 10 9 8 7 6 5 4 3 2 1

TABLE OF CONTENTS

EDITOR'S FOREWORD

In 1949 a West-bound train slowed to a stop on the wide prairies of Saskatchewan, Canada. One young woman stepped off a train onto the dusty August ground and was met by two people who would become very important in her life. Half a century later a similar scene took place. Another young woman stepped from a train into the chilly pre-dawn to meet a couple waiting for her in a warm car.

When I got off the train in Watrous in 1997, I came to visit a woman who hardly seemed like a stranger to me, although we had not yet met in person. I came to the plains for a short time, knowing that I would return home to Virginia at the end of two weeks. When Edna came to Saskatchewan in 1949, she came to start a new life. She was without money, with very few possessions and perhaps too many memories.

I was first introduced to Edna Schroeder Thiessen and her story while working as an assistant in the Archives of the Mennonite Church at Goshen College. At the time I was searching for a topic for my senior research paper – the capstone of my work as a history student. Leonard Gross, a Mennonite historian and my supervisor/ mentor at the Archives, suggested several possible topics, one of which was Edna's story. Leonard handed me a box of tapes and transcripts of an interview he had conducted in 1989 with the help of Rachel Fisher. This interview represented the first effort to record Edna's story, four decades after the events occurred.

While listening to this first interview, I was as fascinated by Edna's story as I was captivated by her lovely accent. I decided to make her experience the focal point for my research paper. Although I handed in my research paper in 1995, my connection with Edna has since evolved into a larger project.

In October, 1996, I spent two weeks on the Thiessen farm, conducting more interviews with Edna, eating her delicious and hearty cooking, and meeting many members of her family and church community in Watrous. This visit helped paint the picture of her experiences in Europe, and helped me understand more fully the context in which the story was finally told.

Since then I have been working on piecing together a coherent narrative from the tangled threads of anecdotes and memories recorded in the various interviews and secondary sources about that period. The intention was to create a readable text that could be shared with Edna's family and community (most of whom have never heard the whole story), and to foster greater understanding about the larger story of Mennonite displacement and emigration following World War II.

I am pleased that after several years of interviewing, writing, and editing, the Edna Schroeder Thiessen Project has now reached its final stages. Edna's memories of despair and hope during the war and post-war eras of 1939 to 1949, are poignant. They afford us rare glimpses into what many Polish Mennonites had to suffer during this time. It is that autobiographical text of Edna's early life which comprises part two, the main body of this volume.

A truncated version of my senior seminar paper, part one of this volume, serves as a general context for Edna's story, both historical and political, as well as religious. The quoted excerpts in this section were taken predominantly from the 1989 interview, and thus do not correspond exactly to Edna's finalized text as found in the second part.

The series of photographs, original documents and a map included in this volume suggest graphically some of the personal moments in Edna's life, contrasting the very distinct eras that she has traversed.

The editing process was complicated somewhat because the final story emerged from multiple interviews with different interviewers. As a result there were parallel but slightly different versions of the same story. In addition, since English was not Edna's first language, there were hints at times of German grammatical constructions which we generally resolved in the editing stage, at Edna's insistence and for the sake of readability. On February 19 and 20, 1999, Edna went over the whole of the final text, carefully, in the presence of Leonard Gross, making numerous suggestions, both factual and stylistic. In this sense, the final text is very much Edna's own. In this final reworking of the entire text, Edna would continuously ask, "Is this good English?" The Epilogue is based in part on conversations between Leonard Gross and Edna, in German (here, translated into English). Edna also went over the Epilogue carefully before pronouncing it "good."

During the final stages Rachel Fisher, Jan Gleysteen and Leonard Gross chose the photographs and documents to be used, wrote the captions, and carried on negotiations with the publisher. I am grateful for their hard work and diligence in seeing the project to completion. I am also indebted to Rachel and Bob Fisher, and to Menno and Naomi Fast, who supplied information about their own experiences in the forties, read earlier drafts of the text, and supplied photographs and journal entries. Jan Gleysteen also read an earlier draft, prepared a map, supplied some photographs, and helped in the design of the book. John Sharp and Dennis Stoesz, too, were most helpful in their support of this project, with the Historical Committee of the Mennonite Church assuming a number of "hidden" costs, but also in providing some essential MCC photographs and documents which add measurably to the story. Special thanks are due the publisher of Pandora Press, C. Arnold Snyder, who accepted this manuscript for publication, and who graciously took time to work through developing problems at every stage, bringing the project to a happy conclusion. And finally, a note of gratitude is also due Edna's family members, and several others, whose generous financial contributions have made this publication possible.

So far, my own life has been tranquil in comparison to the struggles Edna faced during her years in Europe. Working with her story has humbled and inspired me. I have learned lessons about personal strength, the power of faith, and the value of arms outstretched to rescue or to welcome.

There are many brave, strong people who survived the turmoil of war in Europe during the first part of this century. There were also many brave, strong people who did not survive. This story is about one woman who, by the grace of God and the help of many courageous friends and strangers, survived and began a new life in North America. Many times Edna asked me to emphasize that her reason for telling this story is to show how good God has been in her life, and how grateful she is for his love. When I told Edna that I thought she was strong to have done what she did, she responded, "Oh no. Everything I have came from the Lord. He gave me the strength to get through it all."

– Angela Showalter, July 1999

INTRODUCTION

Following the devastation of the Second World War in Poland, the Mennonite Relief and Service Committee (a Mennonite Church organization affiliated with Mennonite Board of Missions, Elkhart, Indiana) made an agreement with the Polish government to begin a food and clothing distribution unit in northern Poland, with headquarters at a rural estate in Pelplin. The MRSC Polish unit was under the auspices of the Mennonite Central Committee and functioned, essentially, as part of MCC and its broad program of European relief work. Wilson Hunsberger, director, arrived in January 1947 and my husband, Robert (Bob) Fisher, and I arrived in March of '47. We were transferred to Poland from Belgium where we had served the previous eight months in food and clothing distributions. Eventually our unit included 8-10 persons from the United States and Canada.

In addition, the Polish government requested other assistance for rebuilding the country, such as tractors and other farm implements. The United Nations Relief and Rehabilitation Act (UNRRA) agreed to send tractors and farm machinery but requested personnel from MCC. These were to be volunteers who had farm experience or training, especially with tractor operation and maintenance. MCC agreed to send 25 volunteers for a six-month period of service, with headquarters in Poznan. Fred Swartzendruber, director, and Menno Fast, assistant director, arrived in January 1947. The work was spread throughout Poland, with these 25 men scattered into many areas. Fred and Menno traveled across the country frequently, and Menno soon discovered there were many refugees from Russia stranded in Poland, including many Mennonites. The Russian government was attempting to locate the refugees and return them to Russia, which many of the refugees feared and dreaded.

At the end of the six-month period the men returned to their homes in the United States and Canada – all except Menno who had developed a great deal of interest in finding Mennonite refugees, many of them in refugee camps, and helping them get to Germany from where they could relocate to other countries. Menno was invited to join our unit and continue his work with refugee involvement. So, although none of us had been given the assignment to work with Mennonite refugees, this ended up being a very important part of our work in Poland.

It was February 1948 when our MCC unit received a short letter from Edna asking for help. She was a prisoner in a labor camp near Warsaw, and was taken each day to work in a store in Warsaw, and returned to the camp at night. Since Bob was planning to take the overnight train to Warsaw to renew our visas, it was agreed that he should try to make contact with Edna at the store where she was working. None of us knew that he would be bringing Edna along back with him.

Edna and I became good friends during those four months she was with our unit. However, our two-year term was coming to an end, and it was time for Bob and me to leave Poland and return to the States. Since Edna had no identification papers, it would have been too risky for her to travel with us, so plans were made by our unit to do all we could to help her get across the border into Germany. On June 6, 1948, Menno wrote in his journal: "In the evening Edna and I took the train at 10:16 (for Szczecin). The Fishers planned to leave a couple of hours later." Bob and I went by train to Warsaw and on to Western Europe. We returned to the States on the *S.S. Veendam*, along with European Mennonites who were delegates to the 1948 Mennonite World Conference sessions in Goshen, Indiana and Newton, Kansas.

It was not until 1961 that Edna and I met again. We were living in Scottdale, Pennsylvania, and had four young children. Edna and Henry were living in Watrous, Saskatchewan, and at that time had four young sons. Henry had hoped to have enough money to purchase a milking machine that year. Instead, in response to Edna's deep desire to visit us, he bought train tickets for the six of them to come from Watrous to Pittsburgh. It was a joyous reunion.

Since then we have kept in touch by letter, phone calls, and visits in each other's homes. On one of our visits to Watrous, we arrived by plane in Saskatoon where Henry and Edna met us. We spent the next week traveling with them by car through Alberta and Saskatchewan. Edna and I occupied the back seat of the car and we had many hours together. This was the beginning of her sharing with me story after story after story about her life during the war years.

Each time we visited in one of our homes, she continued to share more of her life experiences, and I realized then that her story should be written. Her husband and children were also encouraging her to write her story.

I am very grateful to Leonard Gross who became interested in Edna's story and agreed to help me interview her when Edna and Henry came to Goshen for a visit in 1989. This was the first time Edna attempted to tell her "whole story." Soon thereafter, Angela Showalter, a student at Goshen College, also took an interest in the story, focusing her senior history seminar paper on Edna's Polish experiences, an essay which appears in revised form as the first part of this volume. Angela later accepted the intricate task of harmonizing these various interviews into one composite story, which has become the basic autobiographical text of this book. When Bob and I visited the Thiessens in their home in Watrous in 1995, I interviewed Edna for several more hours. Leonard and Angela also made separate visits to Watrous to do more interviewing. I was happy to transcribe the tapes and assist in the editing. Menno and Naomi Fast also went over the text, lending their memory to where Menno had entered Edna's experience, also supplying photos and his journal entries of May 30 to June 11, 1948. Angela wove all these pieces into one story, and she and Leonard then served as the editors, guiding this volume to press. (An "Edna Schroeder Thiessen Collection" has been established at the Archives of the Mennonite Church [Goshen College, Goshen, Indiana] where the interviews with Edna, and other materials, are housed.)

Edna tells her story simply and honestly. It was not easy for her to relive all the horrible war experiences which she endured; she would often weep as she shared her life with us. At the end of the first day's original set of interviews in 1989, Edna said to Leonard and me, "You are helping me. By myself I could not do it. I know the Lord is with us (voice breaking). And this morning I said a little prayer, after which another part of my story came to me. I also said to myself, Oh, the worst part will be over with today. We are moving closer to the light!"

During those years (1939-1948) Edna thought she would never ever laugh again, but the time has come when finally she could indeed laugh again (and we have had many good times together talking and laughing).

Recently when we were visiting in their home, Edna showed me two dresses which are still hanging in her closet: the gray print dress which she wore from the time she left us in Poland until she arrived in Gronau three months later, and the black wool dress which someone sewed for her at Gronau. Edna never once took off the gray dress during her trek to Gronau, and today this same dress gives evidence of the many places where Edna has mended it beautifully (she learned her lessons well in school). The black wool dress was made from the shawl included in the suitcase which Bob took to her when he found her in Warsaw on that 11th day of February, 1948.

– Rachel S. Fisher, Goshen, Indiana (December 1998)

A SOCIETY IN DISINTEGRATION

by Angela Showalter

I. Preface

Beneath layers of history, beneath political structures and religious evolution, beneath any given community's value systems and migration patterns, lie the stories of individuals. Certainly, a complex set of circumstances and influences shape each person's reactions to his or her world. Studying large-scale patterns and trends is, no doubt, useful. However, just as each person's individual history cannot be understood apart from the larger historical context in which it occurs, every communal, national, or religious history must be connected to the actions and experiences of individuals within that larger story.

Within Mennonite history, the story of Mennonites in Europe during the twentieth century has attracted its share of attention. Researchers have been particularly fascinated by the experiences of Mennonites in the Ukraine during the early part of the century. Studies in this area have examined pre-revolution cultural patterns, the persecution suffered under the communists, the flight with the German army ahead of the advancing Soviet troops after World War II, and immigration and resettlement patterns in North and South America. Another area which has gained scholarly attention in recent years is the experience of the Prussian Mennonites. Especially provocative is their involvement with Hitler's National Socialists, the breakdown of their society following the war, and their attempts to flee the Red Army *en masse* across the ice of the Baltic Sea — known as the *Frisches Haff.*

A piece of Mennonite history which has received less attention, however, is the story of the Mennonites in Prussia and Poland during World War II who failed to escape the advancing Russians. Not only did these people see their world dramatically altered by war, but many faced rape, severe hunger, separation from loved ones, forced labor camps, constant threat of death, and loss of identity in a society which no longer tolerated religious differences. Some of the more fortunate managed to escape. Extensive, precise documentation for this region and time period either does not exist, as in the case of war-time rape, or has been largely unavailable to western scholars. However, some of the Polish Mennonites who emigrated to North and South America following the war are still living, and have shared their stories with others. One such person is Edna Schroeder Thiessen, born to a Polish Mennonite family in 1926. She grew up in Poland during the World War II era and currently lives in Watrous, Saskatchewan.

For many years, Edna was unable to talk about her wartime experiences. However, over the years she has maintained a connection with Rachel Fisher, a Mennonite Central Committee (MCC) worker in Poland after World War II, and has gradually revealed pieces of her story to Rachel. In 1989, Edna agreed to an interview with Leonard Gross and Rachel Fisher. In that interview Edna told her story with amazing clarity and rich detail.

This preliminary essay attempts to set the stage for the very personal story which follows. It is my intention that the interplay between the individual experiences of Edna and the larger historical backdrop provide a richly textured portrait of a tumultuous and little-known chapter in the history of the 20th Century.

II. Poland before World War II

During the 375 years prior to World War II, Mennonites developed fairly large and prosperous communities in the region which is now Poland. Mennonites first came to the area from Holland in the last quarter of the 16th century and settled on the Vistula River at its mouth on the Baltic Sea. The land that greeted them was part of a divided and decentralized country.

In general, Poland provided a haven of religious tolerance for the Anabaptist group in the midst of harsh treatment elsewhere. Many of the local officials were more interested in economic prosperity than in chasing heretics. The Polish leaders valued the Mennonites – despite the fact that they were officially unwelcome – because they were skilled at draining marshes and converting them into farmland. For most of their time in the region, Mennonites in the Vistula delta enjoyed social and cultural autonomy, including exemption from participation in the military.[1]

In the 18th and 19th centuries, a small group of Mennonites moved up the Vistula River and established satellite communities in the center of Poland. Eventually, they set up three congregations along the Upper Vistula: the Wymysle, Lemberg and Deutsch Kazun congregations. Edna Schroeder and her family were members of

Deutsch Kazun, which was the first Mennonite church in the interior of Poland. Deutsch Kazun was established in the 1750s, when 23 families acquired land on the Vistula. They, like their relatives in the North, made their area fertile for farming.[2]

Following the Congress of Vienna in 1815, Warsaw and its surrounding areas became a part of the Russian Empire. During the rest of the century, Kazun and Wymysle were under Russian rule, the Lemburg congregation was a part of Galicia in the Austrian Empire, and the community in the North was a part of the Prussian Empire. To what extent these divisions created cultural barriers among the communities is not clear. However, numerous connections continued to exist among them. Congregational structures remained the same, leaders traveled back and forth, and the three southern congregations seem to have faced a similar pattern of cultural assimilation as the Prussian Mennonites.[3]

Like their counterparts elsewhere in nineteenth-century Europe, Polish Mennonites lived in a rapidly changing society, one characterized by Deism, liberal theology and secularism. Partially as a result of these influences, many Mennonites had turned to rationalism more than to revelation. Society was also becoming increasingly cosmopolitan and urban, and Mennonites faced the choice of adapting or withdrawing. In general, Polish Mennonites moved with the changes.[4]

During the nineteenth century, Polish Mennonites gradually moved away from nonresistance. The Prussian Empire brought a more militaristic and nationalistic climate to the region, and made nonconformity more difficult. The issue of whether to support or resist the influences of the Prussian government became highly controversial among Mennonites – since apart from militarism, Prussian ideals closely resembled those which most Mennonites held dear.[5]

When Bismarck pressured the parliament of the North German Confederation to demand universal military conscription in 1867, some Mennonites decided to emigrate. However, among those who remained, cultural separation became less important.[6] Although the congregations in Russian Poland were unaffected by this decree, they felt the effects of northern acculturation and assimilation in congregational issues of their own.

In Edna's own congregation, a near-split occurred in 1881 over the question of allowing the men to wear beards and mustaches, which were a military fashion at the time. Among the Prussian Mennonites military fashions were permitted provided they were put away at the Lord's Supper, a compromise for the congregations in Russian Poland as well. Deutsch Kazun's elder, Heinrich Bartel, however, insisted that the standard be enforced at all times, not only at the Lord's Supper. A majority of the congregation protested vehemently against this adherence to the old regulations.

Several members of the congregation appealed to elders in the Danzig region for help in sorting out the argument. The congregation finally resolved the conflict through an agreement which left the military beard and mustache up to the individual conscience, but required men to shave once elected to serve as teachers.[7] The fact that most of the congregation had strong feelings about the issue, and that it threatened to split the church, indicates the degree to which some members of the congregation identified with the surrounding culture. And their appeal to the leaders in the North shows that the southern congregations took at least some of their cues from the community on the Baltic.

The social situation changed slightly for Mennonites in Poland in 1918, when Josef Pilsudski led a revolution to establish Poland's independence. The new Polish Republic came into existence in the void created by the collapse of the three powers which had divided the land for the previous century.[8] Following World War I and the Peace of Versailles, Poland was divided into three sections: Danzig Free State, East and West Prussia, and the Polish Republic. The following twenty years of independence were ones of increased national pride in the face of outside scorn over the new state.

This new spirit of Polish nationalism naturally made foreign distinctiveness less welcome. Although by the mid-eighteenth century Mennonites had lost some of their original Dutch culture, for the most part they retained their distinctive social, ethical and religious approach to faith. At that time, however, Mennonites in Poland and Prussia were already identifying – both culturally and linguistically – with Germany. Congregations used German for worship, and most Mennonites spoke it as their first language.[9] With the establishment of the new Polish state, these cultural distinctions created more suspicion.

During the interwar period, the Polish government allowed Mennonites broad freedoms, including military exemption. They were also allowed to maintain ties with the communities in Danzig and East Prussia.[10] However, as World War II approached, tensions between Polish nationals and "ethnic" Germans increased. Several Polish-German conflicts emerged during the 1930s over property rights and Poland's educational system. The Polish government made strenuous attempts to acculturate German children, and the German-speaking communities responded by opening private German schools.[11] The tension reached a climax in 1936, with riots erupting against Germans in Upper Silesia, and by the summer of 1939, Polish concentration camps were filled with ethnic Germans.[12]

Into this Poland Edna Schroeder was born on July 22, 1926.[13] Throughout her childhood, her family lived in the village of Secymin, on the banks of the Weichsel-Neiderung River, a tributary of the Vistula. Despite the social tensions around her, Edna's accounts of her childhood in pre-World War II Poland are generally filled with a sense of warmth, protection and happiness. Certainly against the harsh realities of the war years and the following years of Soviet influence, her early life took on a relatively idyllic glow.

Edna was the youngest of four children, but the only child of David Schroeder, her mother's third husband. Her mother's first husband had been killed during World War I, and the second husband had drowned in the Vistula. Edna's oldest brother, Robert, fought for the Germans in France during World War II, and died in Germany in 1973. Her brother, Edmund, died fighting in Russia in 1941. Edna's sister, Emma, and her sister's two sons were living with her mother in 1945 when the Red army "liberated" the area.

Edna's childhood memories include both a sense of learning to work hard and being able to afford time for recreation. In addition to her responsibilities at school and on the farm, she enjoyed playing in the river and riding horses. Like many of their Mennonite neighbors, Edna's family grew mainly fruit, although they also grew vegetables and kept livestock.

Edna's father served as the village's *Dorfschulze*, which was rather like a mayor. This position carried the responsibility of collecting taxes and "giving orders" in the village. Edna remembered that he had acquired some Russian schooling before the Polish liberation, and then had continued his education in Polish schools. According to Edna, he had attained the position of *Dorfschulze* primarily because he was one of the few people in the village who could read and write in Polish, Russian and German. He maintained this position throughout the German occupation (1939-1945).

The religious freedom which Edna's community enjoyed revealed itself in her school. The Polish children at the "Volksschule" were predominantly Catholic, and sat through religious instruction once a week. However, the Mennonite children were allowed to forgo this instruction, leaving for home an hour early on that day.[14]

At home, the Schroeders spoke Low German, but Edna spoke fluent Polish which she learned at school and from her Polish neighbors. As a group, Mennonites were not identified as such with the Polish people, but rather as "Germans" or "immigrants" along with the Baptists and Lutherans. And although Edna recalled being "more Polish than German," she recognized a difference between her family and the Polish villagers:

> We had freedom. I must say we were even a little higher than the Polish people, since when you came in our village you saw the houses, you saw the gardens – all different than the Polish ones. They were usually poor people – poorer than us.
> . . .
> The shopkeepers would have tea and coffee hidden under the counter. They would not sell them to the Polish people because they were too expensive. But when my Dad would come in and ask for a half pound of tea, they would say, "Sure Pan (Mister) Schroeder. We have tea and we will sell it to you." They knew the Mennonites had money to pay for it.[15]

Edna also remembered accompanying her father on trips to sell fruit to a candy-maker in Warsaw. She said that her father and the candy-maker, a wealthy Polish man, were close friends and that she and her father would often stay over at his house when delivering the fruit. This relationship indicates both the family's connection with the wealthier classes and their ties to the non-Mennonite community.

III. The War begins: Poland divided, German territories united

The period of Polish independence ended when neighboring Germany and the Soviet Union made plans to divide the country once again.[16] In August, 1939, representatives from Germany and the Soviet Union met under the guise of trade talks. The result of this meeting was the Pact of Non-Aggression between Germany and the USSR. The pact included a Secret Protocol which laid out plans for dividing Poland between the two along the lines of the Narew, Vistula and San rivers. Almost immediately after the talks ended, Hitler commanded the *Wehrmacht* to attack.[17]

The German attack on Poland in September 1939 was swift and thorough. In a matter of weeks, the fighting had ended, except for pockets of Polish guerrilla fighters. Soviet troops moved in from the east on September 17, thus forcing the relatively weak Polish troops to fight in two directions at once. Even though Britain and France declared war on Germany on September 3rd, they had no time to come to Poland's defense. In the span of a month, Poland lost 60,000 troops and suffered large civilian casualties, and Warsaw was virtually devastated.[18]

During the first few days of fighting in 1939, approximately 5,000 ethnic Germans residing in Poland were killed by "fanatic" Poles. Among the dead were about two dozen Mennonites. Since the Deutsch Kazun congregation was located so close to the Polish fortress of Modlin, this group suffered the greatest during the struggle. Rudolf Bartel, one of the congregation's elders, was arrested by the Poles and executed in front of some members of the congregation.[19] Seven other members were arrested and never seen again, and seventeen members of the congregation were killed. In addition, most of the congregation had their possessions stolen by Poles.[20]

In November 1939, less than three months after the war had begun M.C. Lehman, a North American Mennonite, traveled to Berlin as a representative of MCC to try to aid the Polish Mennonites. Lehman was unable to enter Poland until June, 1940, by which time the congregations of Danzig, West Prussia and Krefeld had already been sending aid to the Kazun congregation. MCC then arranged for a $1,000 grant for the Deutsch Kazun congregation. The German Foreign Ministry allowed MCC to aid Polish war sufferers and former

Polish soldiers in German concentration camps. MCC was required
to work closely with the German Red Cross, and was invited by the
Foreign Ministry to continue relief work after the war.[21]

Although the start of the war initially meant turmoil, including
loss of life and property, many Mennonites celebrated the German
occupation. The memories of Edna and other youth at the time reflect
these general sentiments. Edna's excitement at the arrival of the
German soldiers is evident in her descriptions in her 1989 interview.

> We could not believe that the fighting had ended. Then the
> German soldiers came in. That was so nice! They brought
> chocolates and crackers, and they moved their field-kitchen
> into our garden. They stayed for a week or two. They just
> rested. The fighting was over in our area. It was amazing how
> clean they were. So clean! I can still see those soldiers. I could
> not figure out where they had found all the men. They were
> all same size, the same shape, and the same color. They had to
> have blond hair and blue eyes. Was that ever a picture. And
> they rode the nicest horses![22]

Soon after the invasion, Germany divided its newly acquired
territory into two sections: the northern and western areas were
incorporated into the Reich, and the central and southern areas
(including Warsaw and its surrounding area) were formed into the
General-Gouvernement. Within the first two months of the German
occupation, the Nazis established their racial-division policies in the
Polish territories. All persons living in the occupied areas were
required to register in one of four categories: *Reichsdeutsch* (those
born within the Reich), *Volksdeutsch* (those who could claim German
ancestry), *Nichtdeutsch* (non-Jews, non-Germans), and *Juden* (Jews).[23]
Most Mennonites in these regions were classified as *Volksdeutsch*.[24]

As German nationals, the Mennonites generally received better
treatment by the Germans than the Polish did. While many Poles
were sent to Germany to work as slave labor in factories and mines,
the *Volksdeutsche* were being retrained as "real" Germans. Edna
remembered, "we had it a little better than the Polish people did in
the war. We got a little more food than others."

But Edna added that this privilege only went so far. "We had
to obey," she said.[25] Obedience for Edna and her family meant turning

over a portion of their farm's produce to the German military, as well as complying with the orders for Edna to join the BDM, or *Bund Deutscher Mädel*, a division of the Hitler Youth. "They would call us *Volksdeutsche*. They thought we had German blood. They wanted to train us like German people, to help to win the war," she said.[26]

Today many Mennonites find the level of participation of European Mennonites with the German National Socialist Party difficult to understand. Many ask how Mennonites could have failed to see the problems of that movement. But the problems many people today have regarding Nazism tend to silence the stories of those who experienced it firsthand. In her biography of two Russian Mennonite women, Pamela Klassen argued: "As long as Mennonites cannot face their connections with Nazism, the stories of both men and women who suffered in the war while affiliated with the wrong side will be silenced."[27] Our current view on Nazism is highly colored by hindsight and, for better or for worse, often obscures our ability to see the humanity in the midst of such inhumanity.

Throughout Prussia and Poland during the 19th and early 20th centuries, Mennonites found that the unifying aspect of their identity was increasingly their German language as well as some aspects of German culture.[28] In the 1930s, as Hitler's National Socialist party came into power, many Mennonites found themselves sympathetic to the ideas and agendas of this party. In a recent article historian John Friesen wrote, "Mennonite self-identity was influenced by the recovery of self-confidence, self-respect and pride which Hitler inspired in the German people."[29]

During the 1930s, Mennonite identity also became closely associated with Hitler's ideas of racial purity. Polish and Russian Mennonite scholars set about proving Mennonite racial purity via statistical studies of Mennonite names. Such research showed both a clear desire to be accepted in the Nazi world framework and a view of the superiority of German culture.[30]

Indeed, Mennonites were involved in National Socialism at many different levels. A government official in Marienburg said proudly that Mennonites were getting very involved in the Party, as mayors, officials and government bureaucrats. In addition, many Mennonite youth, like Edna, were involved in the Hitler Youth, and an estimated 900 Mennonites lost their lives while serving in the German army.[31]

John Friesen argued that during their gradual process of acculturation, Mennonites had lost their ability to discriminate, and this loss culminated in their acceptance of the ideas of Nazism.[32] Many pastors during World War II openly departed from nonresistance, arguing that defense of the "fatherland" was harmonious with Biblical teachings.[33] Elder Bruno Ewert of the Heubuden–Marienburg congregation recalled, "Hitler talked in his *Mein Kampf* about 'positive Christendom,' and we trusted in that statement." During the years prior to and during the war, Mennonite intellectuals came to the position that National Socialism had come to stay and they should accept it and make the best of it.[34]

Mennonites also accepted Nazism for pragmatic reasons. Mennonite farmers in Prussia looked favorably upon Hitler's Germany due to the economic improvements he ushered in.[35] Also, as a result of feelings of isolation from the rest of the Mennonite community, many Mennonites in Poland, Prussia and Russia resonated with Hitler's intentions to bring all ethnic Germans home to the Empire, or rather to bring the Empire to the scattered Germans.[36]

Nearly all youth between the ages of 10 and 18 were involved somehow with the Hitler Youth. This included Mennonites. There was the *Jungvolk* for boys aged 10-14, and the *Hitler Jugend* for those between 14-18. For girls, the younger ones (10-14) belonged to the *Jungmädelbund* and for the older girls (14-18) there was the *Bund Deutscher Mädel*. These groups were intended to provide a social outlet for youth, as well as to directly compete with the church by indoctrinating and training them to become good Nazis.[37]

The Nazis' motives for focusing on youth were obvious. By targeting the younger generation for training, the National Socialists could start with relatively "clean slates" with fewer moral strictures to be dismantled.[38] The indoctrination of the youth involved several recurring themes: racial superiority of the Germans as based on "scientific fact"; total loyalty to the state, Hitler and the Nazi party in general; and the idea of *Lebensraum*, or living space, which focused its attention on the need to expand Germany to include parts of Germany's eastern – and shortly thereafter, also western – neighbors.[39]

The camp setting in particular served the aims of the Nazis

well. One of the benefits of the youth camps over training in school or in extra-curricular clubs was the atmosphere. The camps were able to eliminate the "potentially disruptive home environment," and thus intensify training.[40]

The atmosphere in the youth camps could be compared to military boot camps. Activities were highly ritualized, including rising early, physical training and marching, inspections for cleanliness, singing German *Volkslieder,* and the observance of patriotic symbolic rituals.[41] During the war, while the young men and boys served in the military, the girls were called for 2-6 week terms to work at various jobs under the slogan, "Räder müssen rollen für den Sieg," or "the wheels must continue rolling for victory."[42] Edna remembered being sent to Berlin to help assemble Christmas packages for the soldiers, and to East Prussia to help in a hospital for the wounded.[43]

Although they had to obey the German occupying forces, the Schroeders found small ways to resist. One such form of resistance involved Edna's attendance in the youth camps. After she returned from one of several terms with the BDM, Edna refused to return to the camp. When the call came again for workers, she simply failed to report, claiming that her father needed her at home to help with the paperwork for the farm. When a policeman came to look for her, he gave Edna's father the option of paying 50 marks or going to jail. He paid the 50 marks. However, the next time they called for her, she went.[44]

The Germans allowed freedom of worship during the occupation, but the Kazun congregation stopped meeting regularly in the fall of 1939, due to the removal of most of the men to serve in the military. After 1940, Heinrich Pauls, an elder from the Lemberg congregation, began visiting families and conducting individual worship services.[45] Although there was some opportunity for religious nourishment at home, in the youth camps religion was considered unnecessary. It was there that Edna first learned to develop an expression of religion that could be hidden from the outside world:

> They said church was not necessary. I was so used to saying the Lord's Prayer, and there were a few other girls from East Prussia who said we must say the Lord's Prayer together.[46]
> The leaders at the camp told us there is "no God but

Hitler." When I was in that camp, I began to miss church. I thought this especially on Sundays. I wondered why they wouldn't give us a break from the marching on Sundays. On Sundays it was the same thing – marching and singing and shouting, "Heil Hitler" and so on. Until then I did not cry too much. I thought, I will do what the others do, but my heart will not go along completely. They will not take my Mennonite style of living from me.[47]

When the young women in the youth camps reached the age of 19, they left to take steady jobs in Germany or other places in the German territories. Edna managed to find a position very close to her home, working in a flour mill which was being run by the SS. Her cousin had been the secretary in the mill, but was expecting a baby and needed to quit her job. Edna's father arranged for Edna to learn the necessary skills from her cousin, and then take her cousin's position. The skills she learned during her eight months in the mill proved to be very useful to her later during the Soviet occupation.

IV. Memories of Chaos: The Soviet Period

Germany and the Soviet Union had entered World War II on friendly terms, but the events of the war ended their mutual amity. On June 22, 1941, Hitler's armies invaded the USSR and Soviet–held territories in what was code–named "Operation Barbarossa." From then until the end of the war, Germany's control of Poland and a significant portion of the Soviet Union went unchallenged.[48]

In the spring of 1944 however, as Germany's forces weakened, the Soviet Red Army began the "Great Offensive," in which it rapidly gained ground between the Dneiper and Vistula rivers, toward Warsaw. In July, the Polish resistance staged what came to be called the Warsaw Uprising, to liberate the city from the Germans and also keep it from Soviet control. The Uprising failed, left the city completely devastated and further opened the way for the Red Army to make a massive sweep across Poland and Eastern Germany.[49]

In the last few months of 1944, the Germans made a final attempt at holding off the Soviets. To do so they called up all available men to serve for three to four weeks on the front lines, digging trenches and fox holes and building bunkers. These new troops, called the *"Volkssturm,"* included all those men who were previously exempted for farm or civil service.[50] Edna's father was one of the men called up for this temporary service.

The leaders of the Volkssturm discussed plans for evacuating citizens ahead of the approaching Red Army, but they never fully carried out the plans. This failure was partially due to the surprising speed of the Soviet advance, as well as to a lack of organization among the remaining German troops. The second major Soviet offensives took place between the 12th and the 15th of January, 1945, when the areas around Warsaw (including Kazun) were captured almost immediately. Of the thousands of Germans who attempted to escape ahead of the Russians, most were overtaken on their dash for the Oder River.[51]

The mass emigration of Germans from the eastern territories in front of the advancing Soviets (numbers are estimated at around 5 million) was quite sudden and swift, and most of the emigrants did not expect to be permanently separated from their ancestral homes. In addition, the Germans' flight had a more frantic edge than other emigrations because they fled an army which had been goaded into taking revenge on Germans. In the weeks and months before the Soviet liberation, Germans had come to expect the worst from the Russians, and for the most part, they got it.[52]

Accounts of the liberation and the months following paint a picture of a chaotic period during which vandalism, looting, murder and rape were commonplace. In the turbulent postwar atmosphere, the occupying Soviet army joined the Polish soldiers in celebrating the victory by inflicting punishment upon the remaining Germans in the area. Houses were looted, men were taken and killed or sent to labor camps in Siberia, and the remaining women and children were rounded up for questioning and eventually sent to labor camps within Poland or East Germany.[53]

The brutality of the Red Army towards ethnic Germans caught in the occupied territories has often been reported with strongly nationalistic bias.[54] However, this should not disguise the fact that brutality did take place. In fact, Soviet atrocities have been documented in such a broad scope and with such similar patterns of abuse that historians have begun to suspect high–level policies encouraging or even demanding retributive actions.[55]

Almost immediately following the collapse of Germany, countries such as Poland, Czechoslovakia, Hungary, Rumania, and Yugoslavia began massive transfers of ethnic Germans out of the territories. The initial deportation processes were far from "orderly and humane," as ordered by the Potsdam Agreement of July 1945. Typical of war reports, findings on the condition of these transfers vary tremendously. German sources estimate the loss of life during the exportations at 2 million, while a British scholar claimed that the number was "well under 1 million." However, most agree that the conditions improved with time and increased international attention.[56]

Not all of the population transfers following the war were forced, however. Most Germans still living within Poland when faced with the prospect of forced labor or deportation to the Soviet Union realized that their futures had little to offer. In addition, many had relatives in the West, whom they wished to join. During the first few years after the war, more than 200,000 ethnic Germans contacted the Red Cross to be repatriated to Germany.[57]

The Poland which emerged following the war was very different from the Poland which had confronted the occupying forces in 1939. According to the Crimea Conference in February, 1945, the new Polish state would be "organized on a broader democratic basis with the inclusion of democratic leaders from Poland itself and of Poles abroad."[58] While this government, officially titled the Polish Provisional Government of National Unity, was to be an independent nation, in actuality the Soviet Union exerted major influence upon the government.

The governmental structure was not the only change faced by Polish residents. By 1946, Poland's population had decreased by one third from its 1939 levels.[59] In addition, a strong urbanization process removed remaining workers from the agricultural sector.[60] As time went on, the new government eventually realized the benefit of keeping the Germans within its borders to serve as slave labor in a country whose work-force had been severely depleted.[61] From the dust of World War II, Poland's entire social fabric emerged significantly altered.

The Mennonite communities in Poland, the former Danzig

free state, East Prussia, and the Ukraine found that their own social fabric in the postwar years was no longer merely unraveling, but had almost entirely disintegrated. During the war these communities experienced population changes as a result of the men leaving to fight, altered social patterns as a result of the cessation of most religious activities, and new relationships with their neighbors as a result of increased nationalism. But until the war ended, women, children, and the few remaining men stayed together in identifiable communities. When the region came under Soviet influence, however, these communities were scattered forever.

Edna spent approximately eight months working as a secretary in the mill near her home. As the end of the war approached, what she remembered as German "propaganda" about the Soviet Army increased. She was told that the Russians "did things to the girls and the mothers."[62] As the Red army closed in on Warsaw in the winter of 1944-45, the German soldiers gave Edna the option of fleeing with them to the west. But Edna assumed this warning was simply more propaganda, and decided to stay with her parents. In fact, she stayed at work at the mill right up until the Russians invaded.

After the Soviet troops entered Poland, Edna and her family, like many other Mennonites and ethnic Germans, fell victim to the fire of hatred that engulfed the occupying troops and the newly "liberated" Poles. The men who had survived the war were immediately taken prisoner and horribly abused or killed – or they were transferred to Russia, and their fates are largely unknown. The women and children were also imprisoned in large numbers, and, in essence, provided slave labor for the Poles and Russians. Many prisoners were tortured, beaten, deprived of food and water, and kept in abominable conditions. Many prisoners died during this time, and for those who survived, life would never be the same.

V. *"The Light is Coming"*[63]

As time passed, the situation within the newly "independent" Poland became more stable. Those prisoners who had survived the initial chaos were sent to a more organized system of labor camps. On November 16, 1945, the newly established Polish Provisional Government of National Unity issued a decree on the "Creation and

Scope of Activities of the Special Commission for Combating Waste and Economic Sabotage." Under this decree, people who were arrested as "security risks" were given two-year sentences to be carried out in the many labor camps being set up throughout Poland. Most of those classified as security risks had western connections or German origins.[64]

While those who were kept in the camps were seen as enemies of the government, after a couple of years in the camps, they were allowed to seek Polish citizenship. Personal testimonies from this period indicate that the Polish government made efforts to incorporate the German prisoners into Polish society, thereby discouraging massive emigration. Their efforts were quite successful. Approximately 1,400,000 of the Germans who remained within Poland eventually gained Polish citizenship.[65]

However, the decision to become a citizen was not always voluntary or well-informed. A letter from "R.G. from the village of C., district of Sensburg in East Prussia, 11 March 1949," claims that many Germans were baited to Polish citizenship with promises of regaining land and farms and of being allowed to leave the camps and lead a normal life. According to R.G., these promises were false and many Germans were beaten or tortured until they signed.[66] Another account revealed that many Germans in Poland were told that the Americans and British were not going to do anything for them because there were already too many refugees in Germany and the West. Threats of deportation to Siberia were also quite effective devices of persuasion.[67]

As "R.G." observed, the situations of many who acquired citizenship did not improve greatly. Many of those who were released from prison camps were unable to find work despite capabilities, mainly due to the social stigma of being politically unreliable. Those who did manage to find work often received the most menial jobs unless they joined the communist Polish Worker's Party.[68]

Of course one can only guess what sort of life Edna would have been able to lead had she obtained Polish citizenship. A reunion with some of her family in Poland may have been possible. However, the Mennonite community in Poland had vanished, no organized group ever re-formed, and most of the Mennonites had either fled, were evacuated, or remained scattered throughout Poland. Any future for Edna within the borders of Poland would not have resembled her life before the war. Ironically, on the verge of taking Polish citizenship, which probably would have meant permanent residence, Edna stumbled upon the door that led to her freedom.

Edna was one of many Polish and Russian Mennonites who were aided by the Mennonite Central Committee in Poland. MCC, in connection with the Mennonite Relief Committee, had opened a relief unit in Pelplin, Poland (near Danzig) in December, 1946 with the primary focus of providing agricultural and material assistance to the war sufferers.[69] However, they also entered the region with the unofficial goal of contacting remaining Mennonites in the area.

Menno Fast, who later became the unofficial leader of the emigration work, went to Poland initially as the assistant director of the "tractor unit." This unit consisted of a group of 25 men, each of whom was assigned to a state farm in Poland to serve as an advisor on the care and maintenance of the North American tractors which had been donated by the United Nations Relief and Rehabilitation Administration (UNRRA). As Menno traveled throughout Poland visiting the farms, he became aware of the presence of many Mennonites, and the need for establishing connections with as many as possible. When MCC extended Menno's six-month term, he began to focus primarily on cataloguing and contacting all of the Mennonites in Poland.[70]

Word of MCC and its work in Poland traveled by mouth among Mennonites throughout the country. By the spring of 1948, Menno and the other MCC workers had contacted over 200 Mennonites in Poland. In a letter sent to MCC headquarters in Basel, Switzerland, Menno reported the following:

> The total number of Mennonites whom we have contacted in Poland thus far is around 210. There of course is no way of knowing how many more there may be with whom we are not in contact. During the last three months we have received on the average ten new names per month.
>
> The Mennonites in Poland may be grouped according to their nationality at birth as follows: Russian Mennonites 23, Polish Mennonites 97, German Mennonites 36, and those who have acquired Polish citizenship 56. Until now the Polish Authorities have considered all, except the last group, as

Germans, and have dealt with them accordingly; that is, they have disowned them of their properties and placed most of them under the administration of labor camps where they are forced to work, usually without wages. In a few rare cases they may be working privately for peasants who pay them subsistent wages. Others find themselves in prisons where they are practically cut off from the rest of the world.[71]

By July, 1948, Menno had compiled a "complete list of all the Mennonites in Poland." He obtained the names and addresses primarily from relatives in Germany or North America, or from those within the camps who knew of the existence and location of other Mennonites. This list contained 222 people, 82 of whom were listed as members of the Kazun congregation.[72] Although the list was probably quite incomplete, it represented an attempt to pull together the scattered threads of the Polish Mennonite community, and it presents a picture of the mixture of Mennonite nationalities in Poland at that time, as well as their isolation from one another.

Many of the Mennonites on Menno's list were of Russian origin, being among the thousands of ethnic Germans who had been trapped in Poland while fleeing the Soviet army. These Mennonites were the greatest concern of MCC because they were in the immediate danger of being repatriated to the Soviet Union. Much of MCC's work involved presenting lists of Russian Mennonites to Polish officials and attempting to obtain permission for these people to emigrate to the British and American zones of Germany by pleading that their cultural heritage was Dutch rather than German or Russian.

However, this argument caused problems for those Mennonites originally from Prussia and Poland. Whereas the Russian Mennonites had migrated to maintain their cultural distinctiveness, the recent history of the Mennonites in Poland showed that they had clearly accepted a German cultural identity rather than maintaining the Dutch culture.[73] For Polish Mennonites such as Edna, emigration was more difficult since they were wanted in Poland to serve as cheap labor and to provide restitution for their perceived collaboration with the Germans.

MCC's work in Poland became increasingly difficult as U.S.-Soviet relations weakened and the Polish and Soviet authorities became suspicious of its presence. Fast's work with contacting and aiding the emigration of Mennonites was kept on a strictly unofficial level, since his efforts were directly counter to the intentions of the Soviet Government. Fast remembered that often the only way he could make contact with Mennonites was by wearing an armband which identified him as a Mennonite, and by using low German. Once a child informed her mother who was concerned about Russian agents, "you don't have to worry mother, the man speaks low German."[74]

Fast's work with Mennonite refugees caused quite a headache for MCC officials, who were forced to balance the relative worth of his work with the possibility of the closure of the unit. As early as May, 1947, the unit in Pelplin realized that they were being watched by the Polish police. In a letter to Marie Brunk in Amsterdam, Wilson Hunsberger, the director of MCC in Poland, wrote, "Recently we were questioned by the security police and have had visits from the militia. It is evident that we are closely watched and any addition to our number here would cast suspicion on us."[75]

Towards the end of 1947, Hunsberger and other MCC administrators questioned Fast's continued stay in Poland. They recognized that their Polish interpreters had been questioned by the police, and that if Fast's work was discovered, the entire group would be forced to leave.[76] However, he continued working to help Mennonites emigrate until 1949, when the Polish government officially asked MCC to leave the country.[77]

VI. Conclusion

Edna told her story in more or less complete form nearly forty years after it happened. In the meantime, she married and had five sons. She also became a member of a group of Mennonites that was culturally different and in a context far removed from her original one. Her North American home, her family connections, and the passage of time have no doubt affected the way she pieced together her story.

These later influences and experiences have no doubt allowed Edna to re-examine her experiences and to fit her story within the context of the larger Mennonite story. As Pamela Klassen has written, "stories are told with reference to cultural patterns, sometimes in accordance, often in opposition to them."[78] Edna's memory of her life during World War II contained both harmony and dissonance with the larger story which Mennonites, like other communities, use to describe their identity and common values.

While stories such as Edna's play a different role in the recording of history than do documents, manuscripts or church record books, they serve an important function in the understanding of historical events. Stories like hers remind us that at its basic level, history is composed primarily of individuals reacting to events surrounding them. As time moves on and the generation of Mennonites which experienced the events of World War II passes away, it becomes increasingly important to record these stories, and by placing them in their larger context, to understand better these individuals' perceptions of their crumbling world.

Notes

[1] Peter J. Klassen, "Faith and Culture in Conflict: Mennonites in the Vistula Delta," *The Mennonite Quarterly Review* (hereafter, *MQR*) 57 (July 1983): 196.
[2] Peter J. Klassen, *A Homeland for Strangers: An Introduction to Mennonites in Poland and Prussia* (Fresno: Center for Mennonite Brethren Studies, 1989), 45.
[3] John B. Toews, "Mennonites in Deutsch Kasun Make Peace in 1881," *Journal of Mennonite Studies* 4 (1986): 110.
[4] Klassen, "Faith in Culture and Conflict," 194.
[5] Peter J. Klassen, "A Homeland for Strangers and an Uneasy Legacy," *MQR* 66 (April 1992): 120.
[6] Ibid., 121.
[7] Toews, 111-14.
[8] Andrzej Micewski, "Polish Youth in the Thirties," *Journal of Contemporary History* 4 (July 1969), 155.
[9] Klassen, "A Homeland for Strangers and an Uneasy Legacy," 120.
[10] Klassen, *A Homeland for Strangers: An Introduction ...*, 46.
[11] Stephen Horak, *Poland and Her National Minorities, 1919-1939* (New York: Vantage Press, 1961), 128-30.
[12] Ibid., 134.
[13] Edna Shroeder Thiessen, interview by Leonard Gross and Rachel Fisher, 18 March 1989, Tape recording and Transcript, Personal collection of Leonard Gross (Archives of the Mennonite Church [hereafter AMC], Goshen, Indiana). The following descriptions of Edna's childhood are drawn from various sections

of this interview. Exact reference in the interview of each piece of information would become tedious and intrusive. Therefore, one reference to this interview carries for the information throughout this section of memory material.

[14] Edna Schroeder Thiessen, interview by author, Tape recording (by telephone) 16 November 1994, Personal collection of author, New York, NY.

[15] Thiessen, Gross and Fisher interview, 3-4. Throughout the quoted passages, some words, punctuation, or sentence structures have been slightly altered by the author in order to make the passages grammatically correct and readable. Care was taken to avoid altering the intended meaning of the words or sections.

[16] Norman Davies, *God's Playground: A History of Poland*, vol. 2 "1795 to the Present" (New York: Columbia University Press, 1982), 393-95.

[17] Ibid., 433.

[18] Ibid., 441.

[19] Horst Gerlach, "Mennonite Central Committee and the Fate of Mennonites in East Prussia, West Prussia, and Poland at the End of World War II," *Pennsylvania Mennonite Heritage* 11 (April 1988), 18.

[20] M.C. Lehman to Orie Miller, 3 July, 1940, File 2, M.C. Lehman 1940, "CPS and other correspondence, 1940-45," Mennonite Central Committee Collection (IX-6-3), AMC, Goshen, Indiana.

[21] B.H. Unruh and M.C. Lehman, "Report on Relief Work for Mennonite Central Committee," 30 January, 1939, M.C. Lehman 1939, "CPS and other correspondence, 1931-39," Mennonite Central Committee Collection (IX-6-3), AMC, Goshen, Indiana.

[22] Thiessen, Gross and Fisher interview, 29.

[23] Davies, 445.

[24] Gerlach, 17.

[25] Thiessen, interview by author.

[26] Ibid.

[27] Pamela Klassen, 78.

[28] Peter J. Klassen, "A Homeland for Strangers and an Uneasy Legacy," 120.

[29] John Friesen, "Mennonites in Poland: An Expanded Historical View," *Journal of Mennonite Studies* 4 (1986), 98.

[30] Ibid., 98-99.

[31] Horst Gerlach, "The Final Years of Mennonites in East and West Prussia, 1943-45," *MQR* 66 (April 1992), 221-246.

[32] John Friesen, "The Relationship of Prussian Mennonites to German Nationalism," in *Mennonite Images: Historical, Cultural, and Literary Essays Dealing with Mennonite Issues*, ed. Harry Loewen (Winnipeg: Hyperion Press Limited, 1980), 61-72.

[33] Diether-Götz Lichdi, *Mennoniten im Dritten Reich*, in Schriftenreihe des Mennonitischen Geschichtsvereins IX (Weierhof: Mennonitischer Geschichtsverein, 1977), 118-46.

[34] Gerlach, "The Final Years," 231-234.

[35] Friesen, "The Relationship," 66.

[36] Joseph B. Schechtman, *The Refugee in the World: Displacement and Integration* (New York: A.S. Barnes and Company, 1963), 12.

[37] Gerlach, "The Final Years," 232.
[38] George L. Mosse, *Nazi Culture: Intellectual, Cultural and Social Life in the Third Reich* (New York: Schocken Books, 1966), 263.
[39] Norbert Huebsch, "The 'Wolf Cubs' of the New Order: The Indoctrination and Training of the Hitler Youth," in *Nazism and the Common Man: Essays in German History (1929-1939)*, Second Edition, ed. Otis C. Mitchell (Washington, D.C.: University Press of America, 1981), 96.
[40] Ibid., 107.
[41] Ibid., 108.
[42] Thiessen, Gross and Fisher interview, 32.
[43] Thiessen, interview by the author.
[44] Thiessen, Gross and Fisher interview, 23-25.
[45] Lichdi, 6.
[46] Thiessen, interview by the author.
[47] Thiessen, Gross and Fisher interview, 11.
[48] Davies, 453.
[49] Ibid., 474.
[50] Theodor Schieder, ed., *Documents on the Expulsion of the Germans from Eastern-Central-Europe, Vol. I: The Expulsion of the German Population from the Territories East of the Oder-Neisse-Line* (Federal Ministry for Expellees, Refugees and War Victims, Bonn, c1953), 8.
[51] Ibid., 10-14.
[52] Ibid., 21.
[53] Davies, 480.
[54] Marlene Epp, "The Memory of Violence: Mennonite Refugees and Rape in World War II," (an unpublished manuscript presented to the Canadian Historical Association, June, 1994), 1. Used with permission.
[55] Davies, 481.
[56] Schechtman, 12.
[57] Ibid., 17.
[58] U.S. Department of State, "Crimea (Yalta) Conference, February 4-11, 1945 - Protocol of the Proceedings," *Germany, 1947-1949: The Story in Documents*, (publication 3556, 1950), 45.
[59] Davies, 488.
[60] Oscar Halecki, *East-Central Europe Under the Communists*, Publication for the Mid-European Studies Center of the Free Europe Committee, Inc., ed. Robert F. Byrnes (New York: Frederick A. Praeger, Inc., 1957).
[61] Davies, 488.
[62] Thiessen, Gross and Fisher interview, 14.
[63] Ibid., 52. Edna said that although talking about this part of her experience was "heavy," she wanted to continue because, she said, "the light is coming."
[64] Halecki, 479.
[65] Halecki, 45.
[66] Schieder, 340.
[67] Ibid., 342.
[68] Halecki, 263.

[69] Guy F. Hershberger, *The Mennonite Church in the Second World War* (Scottdale: Mennonite Publishing House, 1951), 201.

[70] Fast, interview by author.

[71] Menno Fast in Tczew, Poland, to MCC headquarters in Basel, Switzerland, Letter entitled, "A Report of Our Work Among the Mennonites in Poland for the months of April, May, and June, 1948," Poland, miscellaneous, "Basel - Relief Unit," Mennonite Central Committee Collection (IX-19-3), AMC, Goshen, Indiana.

[72] Menno Fast, "Complete List of All the Mennonites in Poland, July 1, 1948," Poland, miscellaneous, "Basel - Relief Unit," Mennonite Central Committee Collection (IX-19-3), AMC, Goshen, Indiana.

[73] T.D. Regehr, "Polish and Prussian Mennonite Displaced Persons, 1944-1950," *MQR* 66 (April 1992), 251.

[74] Fast, interview by author.

[75] Wilson Hunsberger in Pelplin, Poland, to Marie Brunk in Amsterdam, Netherlands, 28 May, 1947, Refugee Migration - Marie Brunk, "Basel - Relief Unit" Mennonite Central Committee Collection (IX-19-3), AMC, Goshen, Indiana.

[76] Siegfried Janzen in Germany, to C.F. Klassen in Winnipeg, Canada. 27 October, 1947, Refugee Migration - Siegfried Janzen, "Basel - Relief Unit," Mennonite Central Committee Collection (IX-19-3), AMC, Goshen, Indiana.

[77] Fast, interview by author.

[78] Pamela Klassen, 1.

A LIFE DISPLACED

A Mennonite Woman's Flight from War-Torn Poland

by Edna Schroeder Thiessen

CHAPTER 1

BY THE BANKS
OF THE VISTULA

I've lived in Saskatchewan for most of my life. I came here from Europe when I was twenty-three years old, but I felt much older than that inside. When I came to Canada, I built a wall between myself and Europe, and I wanted to keep the memories behind that wall. They stayed there for 40 years, but now I sometimes go behind the wall to bring out the stories for telling.

They are not such nice things to tell. It is a sad story, and a difficult story, but it was wartime, and that is the way things are during a war. I cannot blame one group or another for what happened. The only way I can explain it is that it was war, and nothing made sense. In my heart I have learned to let go and to forgive them all, and I hope the things I tell in this book will be of help to someone.

Most of this story was pieced together from my own memories. Other parts were gathered from other people's memories. During my first year in Canada, my aunt and uncle told me things about my parents that I hadn't known before. When I was a child I didn't care about history and how the pieces of my background fit together, so I didn't always pay attention to the stories. But my aunt and uncle helped me reconstruct some of them when I came here. We would sit up late at night and they would ask me questions about the war, and I would ask them questions about my parents. I learned quite a bit that way. Also, my friends Rachel and Bob Fisher and Menno Fast have helped me recall some details of a part of the story that I couldn't remember on my own.

My story begins in a little village in Poland called Secÿmin, which lay just outside of Warsaw. I was born in 1926, between the two big wars that hit Europe this century. The First World War was over, and the Second was not yet on the horizon. I had two older brothers and an older sister, but I was the only child born to my father, David Schroeder. My mother, Augusta Werman, had two husbands before Dad. Although they were children from my Mom's other husbands, we never called each other "half-sister" or "half-brother." We were just family.

Europeans have frequently asked how I received my "uncommon" name – which of course is quite common in North America. I was named after my cousin, Edna, who lived in Philadelphia, Pennsylvania. But throughout my growing-up years, people often called me Erna.

My mother's first husband, Robert Toews, was killed while fighting against Russia in the First World War. Their house burned down during that war. There was a large military camp nearby in Modlin, so it was in a targeted area during the war. When the house burned, my brother Robert was just a baby. When the fighting got really bad, Mom and another woman evacuated together. They crossed the river and waited where the fighting was not as bad. They were finally able to return a month later, but the house was gone. Only the basement was left.

Since Mom's first husband didn't come back from the war, some other people, including her brothers, helped her put a roof over that basement, and that was her home for two or three years. Then she married Edmund Mathies, who was a bricklayer. He helped her rebuild the house with bricks, so it wouldn't burn down again.

The house had two stories, with rooms on top where we stored our household grain and dried fruit through the winter. We also had a smokehouse where we smoked our meat with the smoke from the stove. Downstairs there were two kitchens – one for use in the summer, on the cooler north side – and one for use in the winter, on the south side.

Edmund died in the Vistula River which flowed past our house. He was crossing the river on his horse. The neighbors saw him go down, but didn't see him come back up. They found him days later, ten kilometers down the river. So my mother was again a widow, six years into her second marriage. By then she had given birth to two more children, Emma and Edmund.

That same river often flooded its banks, despite the dam the first Mennonites in the area had built to contain it. Our house was built up on a high foundation, so we never had much trouble with flooding. But other houses often needed repair or reconstruction when the river swelled its banks. In a way, the river brought my Mom and Dad together.

Dad came from near Kazun. He was born in Leonov, I remember that from his passport – "born in Leonov." This was close to the Wymysle church. He came to our village with his father to help rebuild houses after a flood. Aunt Lydia told me about how Mom and Dad met, and she also told me that my Dad had been Aunt Lydia's first boyfriend! But it was not to be for them. Not long after Mom and Dad got married, Uncle Edmund – Dad's brother – began visiting Auntie Lydia, and soon after that they got married too.

We lived in the fruit belt of Poland, where the land was very fertile. The land was flat, as flat as it is here in Saskatchewan. But the farms were smaller there than they are here, and the whole area was more populated. Everything was closer together. The land beside the river was very fertile, but farther away the farmers couldn't grow as much as we did. Secÿmin was a divided village; there was German Secÿmin and Polish Secÿmin. German Secÿmin had approximately 31 families. Among the Germans, there were many Mennonites, a few Baptists and a few Lutherans. Most of the Mennonites like us lived near the river on the good land. One Polish family lived in our village. They operated our ferry.

The freedom in Poland before 1939 was very much the same as it is here in Canada. We could go to church, and people were friendly. We had Polish neighbors, and a Jewish family lived nearby. We were all friends. But when the war broke out we suddenly became enemies to each other. The Germans were enemies to the Poles and to the Jews and no one trusted anyone. Life was completely different – like night and day.

On our farm we grew pears, plums, apples, cherries and some apricots which my Dad had only started to grow when the war interrupted everything. We also grew some grain and potatoes for our own use. We had nut trees too – a few big walnut trees. Dad had a nursery where he raised new trees for the farm. When a part of the orchard grew too old and stopped producing, the old plants were replaced by hand with the new trees from the nursery. We raised the new plants from our own seeds. The new trees would not produce right away – they first had to be grafted with a branch from a producing tree.

At harvest time we took our fruit to Warsaw to sell, and sometimes Dad let me go with him. That was such fun! We went at the end of the summer, before school started. I had so many things I wanted to buy: books, and wool for knitting and crocheting. We could not buy those things in our village, but we could find them in Warsaw.

Dad usually took the fruit by boat and sold it at a big market where the buyers examined the fruit and bought it for making candy and jam. Sometimes he went by wagon, but it was such a long trip, sitting on that wagon in the wind. I loved riding on the boat, though. We usually spent the night at the home of one of the buyers, Mr. Kwiatkowski. He owned a factory, and Dad knew his family pretty well.

After the fruit was sold, Dad would take me to another market where there were all kinds of things for sale. There was a fish section that smelled so bad! I'm not a fish-eater, so I was always glad when we were away from that section. There was a section where they sold clothes and shoes and books and other things for school. Usually Dad would buy me a doll or some other toy. Mom never came with us; she stayed at home, I guess. The fruit business was more my Dad's job.

One of my jobs on the farm was picking up fruit that had fallen on the ground. I had a little basket where I put the fallen fruit. We sold that fruit to the factory too, and they used it for jams and jellies. I also helped to sort the fruit, separating the good pieces from the ones that were damaged.

I also helped Dad by saving seeds for him. I collected my seeds in a little matchbox, and he paid me something for each box I saved. When visitors came for supper, I would take their plates in the kitchen and try to save every seed from what they had eaten. Mom helped me with that, too. We washed them and laid them out on a paper to dry.

One time I was a very naughty little girl! In the spring Dad and his hired men would go in the garden and spray the trees. They had little scrapers, and they would take a bit of the bark off and scrape the eggs that worms had laid. One day, when Dad and the men had gone into the house for lunch, I decided to help them with their scraping. I scraped so long and so carefully, that I took all the bark off the tree! I "fixed" maybe three or four trees. When Dad found out what I'd done, I got a good licking. I never did that again!

Saturday was pay day on the farm. Very often the workers stopped at the tavern in the next village and drank through the whole night. I began to see how life was for some people. Their families went hungry, but they still had to stop at the tavern and drink with their friends. They would get drunk and play cards, and sometimes fights broke out.

Since Dad had hired help with the farm, and Mom had help in the kitchen, we children did not have to work so hard. We did have some chores to do. After school I would usually work in the garden for a few hours. Sometimes I thought, why do I have to work? I would rather read a book and finish my homework. But Dad said, "Arbeiten ist gesund!" ("To work is healthy!"). When my hands would get dirty he would say, "Oh, when your hands get dirty, that is from work; when your feet are dirty, then you are lazy!" In any case, I was not afraid of work.

I also remember playing a lot as a child. Leah, who was my cousin and my best friend, lived nearby. We played with our dolls and ran around in the garden. We sewed dresses for the dolls, and knitted little sweaters. We bathed them and made little beds for them.

We girls also played along the river, building sand castles along the edge and wading into the water. There was a beach along the river, a little strip of the whitest sand. Leah and I used to swim a lot, and I still remember my red bathing suit. In those days, we didn't use bathtubs as much. We went down to the river with a towel and some soap, and bathed there. Lots of people from the village would come to the river in the evenings before the sun went down to bathe and swim when the water was warm.

One evening a young man, a student at the University in Warsaw, was out swimming in the river near our house. He went down with his friend for a swim, and I guess they went out too far into the middle of the river. I still remember when they brought him out of the water. People stood around looking at him, and someone beat him on the chest, trying to bring him back. But he had too much water in his lungs. He was already dead. So Dad always said, "You can go in the water, but don't go too deep. Just go in until the water reaches your armpits, and no farther."

I loved to swim and paddle around in the boats. I was very good with a canoe. One day I was splashing around in the water near the boat with my hands on the edge, when my feet went under the boat. The water was flowing so hard that it pulled me under the boat. So I let loose my hands, thinking I would swim upstream. But instead, the current pulled me under the boat and brought me to the other side. I think I drank quite a bit of river water that day!

There were two Polish girls from nearby who were also my good friends. Some of the Polish people lived maybe a kilometer or two closer to the forest. They were very poor people. We called them "die Waldmenschen" ("the forest people"). Dad usually hired some of them during the summer to help with the farm, and then we fed them too.

Sometimes Gypsies came into our village and played music for money. They played music like I had never heard before! Mom told us we shouldn't go listen to them by ourselves. She was afraid that they would take us away, or steal things from us. I remember thinking that they were a little bit dirty, but they played the nicest music!

We didn't see any cars in our village before the war, only bikes and horses. People rode bikes everywhere. Just as having the right car is important to young people now, so it was with our bikes. When we had to go to town – seven kilometers away – we went by bike. To ride seven kilometers was nothing for us then.

We also had horses which we used to work the fields. My Dad and I shared a great love for these horses. Sometimes in the afternoons when the work was done, we went on horseback rides together. We called them "foxes," because they were the brownish-red color of foxes.

At Christmas time we were visited by a lot of family – aunts and uncles and cousins, so Mom usually hired a neighbor to help her in the kitchen with the cooking and baking. The neighbor was a German lady named Schuhmacher. She did the washing for the whole village. At washing time she boiled big kettles of water, and it took her two or three days to get everyone's washing done!

People did a lot of visiting back then. Not only at church, at birthdays, and at weddings, but also during the long winter evenings we would sit together and play games. The neighbors would often come and visit. The grown-ups would sit and talk about what they wanted to plant the next spring, and we kids ran around playing. We didn't have a television or a radio. We played checkers using white beans and black beans for the pieces, and we made up other games to play to pass the time. And singing: often, when the work was done we would sing – lots of singing in the evening. We would sit under the chestnut tree and sing and play games.

In the winter we played a game on the frozen lake on the farm. We called it a lake, but it was really just a pond. In autumn Dad would take the boat out on the pond, and stick a big post upright in the middle. When the weather got really cold, the pond would freeze and the post would be frozen solid in the ice. Dad fastened a leather strap with a long stick onto the top of the post. Then we attached a sleigh to that stick and played carousel – swinging around and around on the ice, faster and faster.

On Sundays after dinner Dad would take a nap and we children would have to wait to go out to play. Oh, we could hardly wait! We would spin around and around on the ice, squealing and laughing and falling down in the snow. Then Dad would shovel the snow off the ice, making it smoother. The other adults would come and play too. Mom would come and watch a while, but she usually got too cold and didn't stay very long.

Dad was a hard worker. In addition to running the farm, he was also the *Dorfschulze* or mayor of our village. It was not such a big job, but he was the government representative for our area. He was also sort of a policeman. When there was trouble in the village, they would send for Dad, and he would try to work things out. He wore a badge under his collar, and it was a bad offense to hurt the person wearing the village badge.

There was a lot of stealing going on at that time. Polish people who lived near the woods got drunk and fought a lot. Then they came at night and stole things from our farms. We could not even leave a spade or a rake outside because in the morning they'd be gone. So we kept all our things locked up in a shed when we weren't using them. If someone was caught stealing or damaging property, Dad would try to make it right by returning the stolen items or having the thief work to pay off the damage. But if the offender did not cooperate, Dad had to send for the police to put him in jail for a while.

Dad's job also involved collecting the taxes for the village. He arranged it so that people paid their taxes twice a year instead of all at once. He could make decisions like that. He went to meetings in Sochaczew, where all the Dorfschulzes from the surrounding areas would come together and talk business. Then a representative would come from Warsaw and tell them how much in taxes they were supposed to collect and how many rations the people were allowed to have, or how much money the government would give the people who had suffered damage from the floods.

Dad also lined up transportation for sick people in the village to get to the doctor in Sochaczew. Since there were no cars, everyone had to travel by wagon. Dad kept a list of people with wagons, and each time it was necessary, he went down the list and asked the next person to supply the wagon for the sick person to use.

I always thought that I had the best Dad anyone could ever have. He was so kind. He had a place in his heart for poor people. Often, when they needed some money he would give them some. If they could pay him back, that was good, but if not, it wasn't important to him. As the Dorfschulze, he did a very good job, I thought. He treated people fairly – didn't favor some, or treat others more harshly than the rest. I think that was part of the reason why we didn't flee with the Germans after the war. Dad said that since we had always tried to treat people well, nobody had reason to hate us. But we found out that in war, sometimes people don't need a reason to be cruel.

It was part of Dad's job to take care of the beggars who came to our village and needed a place to sleep for the night. They would come to him first, and he checked his list of people in the village to see whose turn it was that night to give them some food and a place to sleep. Some people would not want to help them, they would say that the people had lice and they didn't want them in their house. If Dad could not find any place for them for the night, he would let them sleep at our house. We would give them breakfast in the morning, and then they'd be on their way.

I liked helping my Dad. He often said, "Come along and help, so you'll know how things are done when you grow up." I'm so thankful he did that. Dad was a hard worker, and I learned from him how to work. That has helped me many times in life. Sometimes I believe that work is the best medicine. I still enjoy being outside. I worked for Mom too, but when Dad called, I went running. I much preferred to be outside helping Dad than inside.

I had a very good Mom. She was quieter than my Dad, very gentle. She was very conscious of *Ordnung* (order). She liked to have everything done on time and done right. She wanted me to keep my room in order, and to be nicely clothed when I went to school. She taught me not to lie to the teacher, the kids, or anyone else, and certainly not to be rough with other children. I think maybe she spoiled me more than Dad did. She was more careful with money than Dad was. She didn't spend very much. However, she did like nice clothing – she was always well-dressed. And she loved jewelry. She was a good mother. She was always there when I came home from school.

At home we spoke Low German, at school I spoke Polish, and at church we spoke High German. My parents and grandparents always said, "Du musst auch Deutsch lernen." That's the mother tongue, they said. But my High German was pretty poor, I must say. We spoke it only at church, nobody used it outside of that. But my Polish was really good. I learned it at school and by playing with my neighbors.

My Dad also spoke Polish and some Russian. Before the First World War our part of Poland was controlled by the Russians and so Dad went to a Russian school. But then the war broke out, and he wasn't able to finish his school in Russian. After Poland won its independence, everyone switched to Polish.

Church was very important to my family. We went to the Deutsch Kazun congregation. I knew from little on up that I was Mennonite and not German. I was conscious of the fact that my Mennonite ancestors were Dutch, not German. We Mennonites were different from the German Germans, living in Germany, but also from those of German ancestry, living in Poland. And that difference was our faith. For example, sometimes I wanted to have an outing with my friends on Sunday. We kids would plan to go for a bike ride or to ride the horses or play on the river. But my Dad would say, "No church? Then, no boating, no horseback riding, no bike riding.

Church always comes first." So we went to church, and then had dinner together. Sometimes we invited visitors to our house, or we went to someone else's house to visit.

We lived pretty far away from the church. We had to go with horse and wagon. Since it was so far away, if the weather was too bad sometimes we didn't go. But our church had communion on Easter, and then we went no matter what the weather was like.

The Drake Mennonite Church here in Saskatchewan is similar to the Deutsch Kazun Church. Some of the families at Drake had emigrated from Poland already before the war in the 1920s. Kazun was traditional Mennonite. But my Grandparents' church – Wymysle – was Mennonite Brethren.

We never hired a pastor at Kazun. Some Sundays different farmers would take turns preaching, and sometimes a preacher visited from Danzig (today, Gdansk). One time an evangelist came from Danzig and held revival meetings that lasted several days.

During school holidays I went to my Schroeder Grandparents' house. They lived very close to the Kazun church. I loved my Grandparents so much! We were really close. For a while I was their only grandchild, so it was extra special to be with them. My Grandpa's name was Peter, and Grandma's was Eva. Her maiden name was Bartel. Most of the Mennonites who went to Deutsch Kazun were either Schroeders, Bartels or Nickels, with a few Kliewers thrown in.

Grandpa would take my hand when it was time to go to church, and we would take the short cut. The short cut was a footpath that went through other people's orchards, but Grandpa knew the people well enough to know that they wouldn't mind.

My Grandma was a saved person. From Grandma I learned to pray aloud, not just silently like we did at home. She would cook breakfast, and then when we got to the table she would pray first, even before the others would come. I would stand close to her or sit on her lap while she prayed. Grandpa was a good man, and he lived his life by good deeds. He did good things and helped the poor, and I think he thought he was good enough to go to heaven. But I don't know if he ever got saved.

At my Grandparents' church we didn't have Sunday school. But I remember that some people started organizing afternoon prayer groups. We children went to "Kinderstunde," and the adults met in homes for prayer. They read the Bible and prayed out loud. We kids could hear them praying from where we played outside. Most of the words were so big that I couldn't understand what they meant.

My mother and father taught me to live according to the Ten Commandments and the Lord's Prayer. Every day I said the Lord's Prayer before I went to school. That was my prayer. And they taught me verses from the Bible. And through all the war years that I didn't go to church, these were the things that stayed in my mind. When we couldn't go to church, I missed it very much. Something was just missing. But I often said the Lord's Prayer to myself.

Later, as I walked through Germany, I passed by many churches. Often I heard the bells and went in just to look around and feel God. I remember looking up at Jesus on the cross, and I knew that he died for me and for the rest of us here. They were mostly Catholic or Lutheran churches, but I didn't care what kind they were. I missed church so much!

After dinner on Sundays, Grandma and I often went to the graveyard. My aunt was buried there. Her name was Bertha, and she had died when she was only 17. Grandma would pick flowers and give me some. Then we would lay them on the graves and talk. She had other relatives there – perhaps her parents. We put flowers on many graves.

When it was time for school again, they took me across the river to Modlin, and they bought me clothes. I remember one outfit: it was all red with polka dots, red shoes and red socks, and a red school bag. Red was my Grandma's favorite color.

My first year at school stands out so clearly in my mind. It was a very exciting time for me. Everything was so interesting and there was always a lot of school work to do. I loved going, so much so that at the end of each day I couldn't wait for the next day to start! We learned geography and counting, sewing and cooking. Dad would tell me, "Even though we are farmers, we can never learn too much. We need education simply to know." I have lots of things from my Dad, including being interested in a whole world of things.

Our school was in a nice building, right across the lake behind our farm. All the classes were separate, and there was a big dining room with loud speakers and a radio. We went to school six days a week. In the lower grades we came home at 2:00, but the upper grades stayed until 3:00 or 3:30. Religion class was usually the last class of the day. Most of the Polish children were Catholics, and they had to stay for the religion classes, but we "Germans" and the Jewish children did not. We were allowed to go home.

I was a happy child. But the war was coming closer and closer to my life. I heard people talking about politics, but I didn't pay much attention. I thought it had nothing to do with me. I thought that we all lived together in our village, and people were people. I never thought that the differences between us would cause problems. But then everything changed. I did not know it at the time, but those dark war years would turn my childhood freedom into a distant memory.

BENEATH PLUM TREES

I always thought that the Polish people liked us Germans. But closer to the war, when they overheard us speaking German, they started saying mean things about us. They said that the Germans would cause a war, and they started picking on us. "You are a German," they would say, "You are a *Hitlerrowicz* (a Hitler person)." We heard those things even before the war began, so we knew things were changing.

I remember there was some hostility towards the Jews, too. There was one Jewish family in our village with a boy who was close to my age. The Polish children didn't like him very much. He was smaller than the other children, so the boys pushed him around and picked on him. When we were playing outside they would hit him with the ball and do other unkind things to him. I thought those boys were mean. Sometimes I stuck up for him, but other times I didn't. Sometimes for lunch he had just a piece of dry bread, so I would bring him an apple or pear and stick it in his pocket or his desk.

The Jews in our part of Poland weren't farmers. They ran businesses – barber shops, grocery stores, or tailor shops. The Jewish family in our village, Abram and Surra (Sarah) Wolf, were tailors. Mrs. Wolf sewed clothing for the ladies, and Mr. Wolf sewed clothing for the men. Back then we couldn't buy ready-made clothes from stores, everything had to be sewed from material that we bought.

I remember going to their house to pick up a dress that I had Mrs. Wolf sew. I went on a Saturday, and when I arrived they were still saying their prayers. We could not talk to them until they had finished. I remember at Passover they ate unleavened bread, and Mr. Wolf gave me some of it to try and some to take home to my parents.

From as early as I can remember I believed that we children were all the same. But closer to the war, things started to change.

There was hatred in the air. The lower class Poles started killing people. We called them drunks or robbers. They went out at night to steal things, and they lived on what they took.

The killing started in Łodz, a city about 60 kilometers from Secymin. There were many German immigrants in Łodz, and many silk factories, most of them owned by Germans. The Germans there were richer than most of the Polish people. The violence began because the poor people wanted to pull the rich people down. Of course there were some wealthy Polish people, but not very many.

The war really started one day while we were in school. Our Polish teacher usually had the radio turned on during our lunch time. We children didn't listen very much, but she listened to the news while we ate. On that day, in the middle of lunch she switched the radio off and came over to speak to me. She was friends with my parents – especially my Dad, since he was the mayor. And she was my friend too. She hugged me and said, "Edna, now our ways will part. Never forget the Lord." She was a Polish Catholic, and I guess she knew that during the war we wouldn't be able to be friends openly. Then she announced to the whole school that we all had to go home.

There was so much tension in the air that day! Once outside we could see the airplanes flying overhead and bombs falling on our land. The war had just started! We all ran home as fast as we could. Our farm was one and a half kilometers away, and we had to go around a little lake which was between the school and the farm. So I was running around the lake when three German bombers came – one in front and two more behind. They made huge craters in the ground all around us, but we weren't hit. When we arrived at home we could see the craters everywhere. And then, suddenly, all was quiet; there were no more bombs. When I got home, I was out of breath and very scared. Mother was busy putting *Federbettdecken* (feather blankets) in our windows so the glass wouldn't spray into the house. She had learned her lessons well some 20 years earlier in the first war. She was very quiet. It was time for dinner, but nobody could eat; we were all too frightened.

A few days into the war the police came to our house and told Dad to come outside. They had gathered all the German men from the village, and said they were needed to dig trenches for the war. But they didn't dig any trenches. Instead, the police chased Dad and the other men to the next village, where they rounded up more men. People said there were about 300 men altogether, but we found out later that there may have been more than 700!

Dad was gone nearly six weeks. When he left, he was energetic, with lots of life. When he finally returned, he had nearly wasted away. He was bruised and dirty and looked like a skeleton. I gave him a hug and a kiss, but he was just skin and bones. He did not seem like my Dad. He could not talk at first. His hair was so thin and straggly, and he stood there like a wild man – the result of horror and hunger. Mom tried to feed him, but I guess his stomach was so empty that he had to take it slow. He said he couldn't eat much. It took him a long time to regain the weight he had lost, and for a long time, he didn't say anything about what had happened to him. But eventually he told us the whole story.

The Polish police chased them all the way to Lemberg (today, Lvov), near the Russian border. They made them run, they were not allowed to walk. Days and nights they ran without stopping for food or even water. The police were on horses and bikes, and they pushed the men towards the Russian border, away from the oncoming German troops. The Russians were advancing on Poland from the east, and the Germans were coming in from the west. Russia and Germany were trying to carve up our country like a turkey.

None of the men knew where they were going. They just ran for days, with no food or water. Dad said the worst thing was their thirst. They couldn't even stop to drink! One by one, some collapsed and died. Later we heard that the Polish people were also chasing Germans into the forest to shoot them. Apparently this was true, because when the war was over, they found mass graves full of the bodies of Germans.

Dad told us that the sky turned blood red from the spotlights the Poles used to find the planes to shoot them down. These spotlights lit up the whole sky. They were surrounded by fighting. The Germans had a kind of a cannon that when it was fired, there was a flame that burned everything. The trees and the grass would burn. One evening when the fighting was especially fierce, there were tanks in the woods all around them, and there was so much shooting and bombing. The tanks ran over everything, even civilians in the streets. The front lines had come so close together that Russian and German bullets were flying in all directions, killing many within Dad's dwindling group, along with some of the Polish guards. The rest of the guards finally all ran away.

Then Dad decided he should just run for his life. "They will kill me anyway," he thought. So he broke away from the group and ran onto a potato field and burrowed himself into a ditch between the rows, digging with his hands as deeply as he could. He heard the shooting all night, the machine guns and cannons and tanks. He even heard bullets skidding across the dirt in the field, so close to his head. But he was safe – he was almost completely covered with dirt.

The next morning, everything was quiet and still. There were no soldiers shooting, no tanks moving – only the dead lying on the ground around him. So Dad dug himself out, got up and hid in the woods nearby. After a while he walked to a nearby village. He begged for some food, he was so hungry and thirsty. But he didn't know where to go from there. Was he in Russian territory, or Polish, or German? He thought he should wait a little bit and figure things out.

He met two Polish women whose husbands were off fighting in the war. Pretending to be Polish, he asked them if he could stay with them and help with the chores. And they agreed. Everything was quiet then, and he just stayed and watched. After a week or two, there were Germans everywhere, so he said he felt safe enough to return home. They had been chased perhaps 700 kilometers from home, so now Dad had to walk the same distance back. Trains had been bombed, but even if they had been running, he had no money for a ticket.

When the fighting was finished, women from our village and the surrounding ones boarded a train and went somewhere to identify their dead husbands and sons. My Aunt Otilia – Leah's mother – found her husband, Uncle Heinrich, because she recognized his boots and his gold teeth. Many men were killed, and it was a very sad time. But by that time, the Germans were in power, so things were better for us.

We now call this time the "six-week war," when the Germans were coming into Poland. During the fighting before the Germans took over, Polish bandits came and stole food and other things, and even killed people. They would come into a village and shoot any remaining cows and pigs belonging to the farmers. There was very little food, but they would come and take whatever we had.

Some nights we were so scared of the bandits that we would put on many layers of clothes and sleep outside in a haystack or under a hedge. Other nights we slept outside for fear that soldiers would come during the night and burn down our house, or do something to us. At first we hid in the basement, but Mom thought that when the airplanes came and dropped bombs, the bricks would fall and kill us. So then we went outside.

It was September and the plum trees were heavy with plums. We crawled beneath the branches to hide, but we knew the tanks could run over everything – trees or no trees, it didn't matter. So we felt like we weren't safe anywhere.

Most of the killing in our village by the Polish people happened right before the Germans entered. They said, "We have to get rid of the German colonists so they will not eat our Polish bread anymore." We could not understand what that meant. Before the war we were living here together. Nobody hated anyone else, we lived in freedom. But now it all changed, and we couldn't understand why.

My sister came to our house a few weeks into the fighting. She had two little boys, and she left them with us for a while. She had hired workers on her farm, and she went back to help them get the harvest in. They had rye fields and cherry trees, and they wanted to put everything into the barns. They worked very hard, but soon everything was destroyed anyway – the barn burned down during the fighting.

Our village was only partially destroyed. The biggest problem was that the gardens and the fields were badly damaged. When the German tanks came through, they rolled over everything: ditches, fruit trees, potatoes, and sugar beets. It was like thunder was rolling through the country. We had very little food left for the winter. Most of the fruit was destroyed, so Mom tried to make jam with even the damaged fruit that was left. But we didn't have sugar, so the jam rotted.

Since we were very close to Warsaw, the fighting was very heavy around us when the Germans came. Sometimes we could see the Germans on the other side of the river, while Polish soldiers were still stationed on our side. When the tanks came through, we were relieved when they kept rolling past because that meant that the front was farther away. If the tanks stopped, that meant we were right on the front lines. Sometimes airplanes circled overhead, dropping bombs. Usually they doubled back and flew low enough that they could shoot with machine guns. They shot at everything – men, women, children, animals. That was their aim, to kill as much as they could.

Polish soldiers were running everywhere. At night we heard them running, and during the day they would come to us for food. Mom would give them milk from the cows and fruit from the trees, and then they would go on. One night we heard them running and running all night. In the morning, very early, before the fog had lifted, Mom and I looked out the window and saw different horses and different soldiers everywhere. Mom said, "I think these must be the Germans."

The German soldiers asked us if we had seen any Polish soldiers, or if there were any hiding in our house. Mom told them that we had heard them running all night, but we didn't know where they were now. I remember the Germans' horses – such beautiful horses!

Mom said to the officers, "Werden Sie es diesmal auch so machen, als Sie es im (ersten) Weltkrieg gemacht haben?" Which means, "Will you do it like you did in the (First) World War?" She was a brave woman!

The officer said, "Aber Frau!" but they just turned their horses and rode away.

I said to Mom later, "Maybe you shouldn't have asked him that!"

"Well," she said, "I was really disappointed in them in the first war. Things were good here in Poland before the first war. But the Germans came and messed everything up, making us enemies with the Polish people, and then they left."

I thought my mother was very brave for saying what she did. I'll always remember her standing up to those soldiers.

"VOLKSDEUTSCHE"

I must admit that I was relieved when the Germans took over. I was not happy because they were in power, but because I was glad that the fighting was over and we finally had something to eat. During those six weeks of fighting life was so difficult. We did not have food, and robbers came and took everything. So at least when the Germans came, there was order and there was food.

While there was still fighting just to the east of us, the Germans came and set up a kitchen in our garden. They were pushing towards Warsaw. I still remember how good everything smelled and how happy I was that there was food! I was very young, but I would go close to the soldiers and talk to them a bit. They asked Mom and me if we wanted to have some of their food. We were scared – the war had just started, but already we had learned to be afraid of people, to be cautious. But one of the cooks said, "Come, come. Open your apron and I will give you some food." And he put some chocolates in my apron, and crackers – I had never seen crackers before! I had seen chocolates, but not crackers. And I said, "This is all for me?" And he said, "Yes, it's for you, just go and give your mother some too."

Later he told us to bring back a container, and he would give us some soup. He made the nicest soup. It was some kind of barley soup, and it smelled so good! The Germans had a big army wagon where the cook kept his supplies. The other soldiers sat around cleaning their rifles, or shaving, or cleaning their shoes. They stayed on our land for three or four days, and then they received orders to move on. But at least we had good food for a few days while they were there.

When my Dad came back, and after he had regained some of his strength, we began to harvest as much of the food as we could from what was left. The tanks had destroyed so much, there wasn't much remaining. In some corners there were patches of wheat still standing. We gathered as much as we could so we would have a little flour for the winter. We didn't know how much the Germans would give us, or if there would be any food to get us through the winter.

We had scythes to cut the wheat by hand. Of course, we didn't have any hired help. It was just the three of us, and we worked as fast as we could.

We didn't know what would happen to us when the fighting was over. The Germans were still fighting, and Dad said we must be prepared for whatever happened. So Dad cut the wheat, and Mom made it into bundles, and I helped Mom. We took the wheat and lined it up into similar-sized bunches, and twisted it into a tight bundle. It was so different from before. Usually we had hired people to help, but now it was just the three of us in the fields. We used to have a horse to bring the bundles in from the fields, but now we had to carry them. Dad would take some bunches in his arms, and I would take a couple, and Mom a couple, and we carried the bundles into our shed for the winter.

We picked fruit too. It was very ripe, since it hadn't been picked during the six weeks of the fighting. So we picked as much as we could, and dried a lot of it. That also helped us get through the winter. I guess Mom and Dad remembered from the first war that when war comes, the food disappears.

In the cities the situation was even worse. And the Poles got even less to eat than we did. They were really hungry! They came on our farms and begged for potatoes or anything we could give them.

On Sundays we prayed together as a family – there was no church anymore. Many of the men were killed, and those who were left had to go fight for the Germans. So we stopped having church. On Sundays Dad read from the Bible and we prayed. "Lord, we are tired of this war. Please bring an end to it." Everyone was tired of the war.

The years from 1939 to 45 were war years, but they were not as difficult for us as they were for the Polish people or the Jews. The German soldiers and officers gave us more freedom. They did not care if we were Mennonites or Baptists or Lutherans, we were German blood, and that's what mattered to them. Also, there was not much shooting or bombing during that time. The Germans were in control, and life was different from before, but it wasn't as scary as those first few weeks when the fighting was all around us. At this time my Mom reminded me to continue respecting the Jews. She said, "Just love them like we did before the war; and don't be bad to the Polish, they are good people." During the early months of the German occupation when there was almost no food, we sometimes would take bread and milk to our Jewish friends, the Wolfs.

When the German airplanes flew over us towards Russia, they just kept flying. They didn't drop bombs on us, of course. I remember standing outside and watching them fly overhead. They flew like geese – one in the front and the others in a V-shape behind. Usually we didn't hear the bombs. But later, when the Germans were retreating and the Russians were approaching, we could hear the cannons and the boom of the bombs. From 30 or 40 kilometers away they sounded like thunder. And the windows would shake sometimes when they dropped the bombs. Even now, when I hear thunder, those bombs are in my ears, and each time I am terrified.

New passports were issued immediately after the Germans took over, and ours read "*Volksdeutsch.*" Everybody had to have a passport. We had blue ones, and I think the real Germans had red ones. We were *Volksdeutsche* because we were considered Germans, but we weren't born in Germany. Those who were born in Germany were called *Reichsdeutsche*. Everyone had to have his passport with him at all times. I remember going to Modlin to get some ration cards for food. Even though Modlin was only 12 or 13 kilometers from our farm, on the way there were several roadblocks. At each one I had to show my passport before the guards would let me pass.

In 1940 life suddenly took a hard turn for the Jews. We had been friends with these people who in our eyes were just like anyone else. The Germans left them alone at first, then forced them to wear the yellow star. After this, people would pick on them and push them around. In the stores they received only the leftovers, if that. Around this time, Abram and Surra Wolf and their family began coming to our house regularly in the afternoon, and Mom would feed them. They stayed longer and longer into the evening, and even into the night sometimes, so that they would not be in their own home, for fear that the Nazis would take them away. They knew from elsewhere that Jewish families were being taken away; their turn might come at any moment. Other local families also hid Jews in this manner.

The time the Wolfs spent in our home may well have delayed their "capture," with the Nazis going to their home only to find it empty. Through all this, Dad and Mother may well have been placed on the SS "schwartze Liste" (black list). The moment finally came, however, when the German police – the SS – came and took away the Wolf family. We assumed the police had come in the early morning while everyone was asleep, knocked on the door, and gave them the usual three minutes to gather a few things, with the police not even permitting them to put on proper clothes. The Jews always had to go just as they were, even in their night clothes.

In the beginning, we didn't know where they were taking the Jews, they were just gone. But later we saw what they were doing with them. Even I saw. We had to travel back and forth to Modlin to get papers and rations, and there was a train going from Warsaw to the west, which passed through Modlin. The Germans were taking the Jews and other prisoners to camps in Germany on these trains. They loaded them like cattle, crammed in the train cars. People cried and looked up to the heavens, children wailed. But what could we do? I just pedaled my bike and looked at them on the tracks and wondered what would happen to them. There were old people and young people, some blondes, some with dark hair. The Germans just loaded them all up and moved them out.

Eventually we found out what they did to the Jews, but not in the beginning. We found out that the Germans had built a camp in Warsaw, a ghetto, where they kept the Jews, but we had no idea what they were doing.

At first, they didn't take the Polish people away. But after about half a year or so, when the government was set up in Poland, they took the Polish people to work in Germany and they brought in teachers from Germany for our schools. My Polish teacher moved back to her home city, Sochaczew, 35 kilometers away. The Polish storekeepers had to move out and a German would move in to reopen the store. The Jews were all taken away by that time, and the Polish people who remained weren't allowed to go to school. Only us German people were allowed to go to school.

There was a narrow-gauge railroad about three kilometers from our house. It was built to haul sugar beets in season, but it carried passengers and mail as well. Farmers used to store beets in a building by the tracks before they were shipped to the sugar factory in Sochaczew. Since our schoolhouse had been burned in the fighting, the Germans set up a school in this old sugar beet building. But soon after we started having school again, Polish partisans, hiding out in the forests, came at night and destroyed things, burning and breaking whatever they could. So the teachers got scared and went back to Germany. School lasted only a few days. By the third day of school, our teacher had also left.

In the beginning the Germans ordered only our young men to fight – ages 18, 19, up to 24 or 25. But later on, when so many men got killed on the front, the Germans didn't have enough soldiers. So they took our older men, 40, 45, 50, even older. They forced all of them to fight. But my Dad stayed in our village. He didn't have to fight since he was the *Dorfschulze* and also because he had been injured. That's quite a story too!

When the Germans came in, they made a law that if any German – *Reichsdeutsche* or *Volksdeutsche* – wanted the house or farm or job of a Polish person, he could inform the German officers, and then simply take it. And the Polish people who had been living on that farm would have nowhere to go. We thought of this law as a kind of poison for us. It caused such hatred! I think that's partly why things were so bad for us after the war. Anyway, that happened to our Polish neighbors. They were such a nice family! The father was the one who ran the ferry across the river. And their daughter Zofia worked for us in our house.

During that time, if the Polish young people didn't have jobs, they were sent to Germany to work in the mines. So our neighbors decided that they would rather have Zofia work for us so she wouldn't have to go away. One of the other children worked in Warsaw, and the others were hired out all over to the local farmers. The new German government had issued orders that Poles were not to eat with Germans at the same table, but we did it all the time. Zofia, and the two Polish men that we often hired, ate regularly with us at one table.

There was a man from the village, Mr. Toews, who decided he wanted to take over our neighbor's job and house. He was a kind of a drunkard, and when he was drunk people were scared of him. Instead of keeping his own house in order, he let things fall into disarray. But now, since the Germans gave us the right to take whatever we wanted, he decided he wanted our neighbor's farm.

Mr. Toews was often drunk, and my Dad was a bit afraid of him, I think. One day after Mr. Toews had been drinking, he staggered to our neighbor's house, opened the doors and yelled, "Get out, get out! I'm moving in here." One of the children came running to our house and told Dad what Mr. Toews was doing. So Dad called another man to help him settle Toews down. Dad thought Toews should not do such things when he was drunk. If he was going to do it, he should be sober.

So Dad and the other man went over to talk to Mr. Toews. When Dad got there, Toews was so angry that he started fighting them. He swung and hit my Dad in the face. As he swung, his fingernail caught my Dad in his right eye. Later Dad said, "As soon as I hit the floor, I knew I had lost my eye."

The other man who was with him calmed Toews down, and brought Dad home to us. Dad's eye was burning and stinging so much. So they hitched up a wagon and took Dad to the doctor, who sent him to Litzmanstadt (today, Łodz) for treatment. They came home and got my Dad some clothes. Litzmanstadt was 60 kilometers from our village, so he went by train. He stayed in the hospital for ten days or so. They thought they could save his eye, but they could not. And that was one of the reasons he didn't need to fight for the Germans. He needed his right eye to be a soldier.

We were glad he could stay at home, but so sad that he lost his eye. I remember one day I sat on his lap, eating an apple. I looked at his eye and asked him if it bothered him. I shut my eye to imagine what it was like, but then I just saw my nose.

Dad said, "When you get used to it, you don't see your nose so much anymore." He didn't mention it much after that.

Fighting and stealing and other bad things were always happening in the villages at that time. Dad said it was because of the war. Everyone was just a little crazy and fed up with the war. They were hungry and scared, and exhausted.

The German police set up a base in Sochaczew for governing our region. My Dad was still the elected village Dorfschulze, and he had even more responsibilities than before. Rationing was taken very seriously, and so mountains of paperwork accumulated. People who had cows or chickens for their own use had to give a certain amount of milk and eggs to the government, "to help win the war." Everybody was required to participate. And Dad had to oversee this whole process.

During this time we could not drink whole milk – we had to send the cream away to make butter, which was then sent to the soldiers on the front lines. Women who were pregnant and children were allowed a certain amount of whole milk, but everyone else had to drink milk that had the cream taken off. If one farmer couldn't deliver enough food one week, everybody in the village had to pay a fine. So we helped each other even things out. If our chickens didn't give us enough eggs, we went to the neighbors and they gave us a couple extra. And we did the same for them.

After the fighting, many German officers and civilians moved into our area. The officer who was just above my Dad was a German Amtskommisar. He was so strict! We thought he was really a Hitler person. His life's purpose was to serve the Nazis. Dad was a little afraid of him, I think. We had to be very careful around him. If we didn't behave, we would be treated exactly like the Polish people, or even the Jews, so we had to listen.

Dad said this man was *falsch*. He appeared to be nice, but underneath he was searching for ways to get us into trouble. He came to our house for lunch sometimes, when he was meeting with Dad about something. One day he sat down to eat and noticed that we were drinking milk for lunch. He picked up a glass, tasted it, and said, "What is this? Drinking whole milk for lunch?" So he gave us a fine for using whole milk when we weren't supposed to, even though the milk had come from our own cows.

Between us and Warsaw the Germans put up a border. They called the area within this border, around Warsaw, the Polish Government. We called it the Protectorate. During the German occupation, we never went to Warsaw. There was a checkpoint which we couldn't pass through. I never had a chance to ask anyone why we weren't allowed inside. We even had to send our fruit in the opposite direction, to help with the war.

We thought that once the fighting ended, things would return to normal. But everything was different. The Germans built barracks close to our village. There were maybe 100-150 men staying there. Their job was to guard the border between us and the protectorate to make sure that we didn't go inside, and that the people inside didn't go out. They stayed there for a year or so.

During this time the Polish partisans would sometimes come at night and shoot at the barracks with machine guns. And then in the mornings people would be so nervous, wondering what would happen next. We were maybe only five kilometers from where the barracks were. Soon after the partisans attacked, the Germans moved a bit closer to Warsaw, and they were reinforced with more and more weapons.

That was a very dangerous time for us! We never saw the partisans. But they would come at night and loot our things. One time they cut the heads off our pigs, and in the morning we found only the heads. Another night they stole our cow. They came to other farmers and robbed them too.

Soon after the occupation began, the Germans started sending all ethnic German young people to training camps. We called them camps, but the Germans called them *Erholungslager*. Erholung was the word for a place you went to when you were a bit run down. It was like a retreat center, I guess. Since we were born in Poland, grew up like Polish citizens, and went to Polish schools, we didn't know much about Germany or Hitler or the Nazis. So the Nazis wanted to take us in and teach us to be real Germans. They believed that since we were Germans, we should think and act like Germans. Hitler wanted all the young people growing up to have faith in him and in what he was doing. "There is no God but Hitler, Hitler is your God!" they said. They pounded this into us, again and again.

A letter came in the mail each time I had to go to a camp. The letter was called an *Einladung*, or an invitation. But it was an order, not an invitation! We had to go. A big pile of these papers would come to my Dad since he was the Dorfschulze, one for each German girl in the village. Then I would ride on my bike from one house to the next to take them their papers.

The first camp we went to wasn't very far away from home. It was maybe only 30 or 35 kilometers away, in Płock. We took a bus to that first camp. The bus picked us up about four kilometers away, across the river.

We had to pay for our transportation to the camps, but then they paid us back. We also had to bring a little spending money. But otherwise, the government paid for everything we needed while we were there. There was never much to buy at the camps, some fruit or some cookies for snacks. In Płock there was a Polish bakery where we bought some cookies to munch on in the evenings. For that we had to have spending money.

At each camp they taught us to read and write German, and they taught us German history, including how the Nazi Party was formed. For me it usually went in one ear and out the other. I was not very interested. They also taught us to be good cooks, to save, to be good housekeepers – everything as a part of the war effort. Aside from this Nazi business, the camps were not bad. We had enough to eat – good food – and we had rights.

Most of the camps were held on large pieces of land – huge farms which had been confiscated after the six-week war. Usually one or two women would come to teach us. They were all so energetic, like soldiers! They must have brought girls from all over Poland, from the cities and the villages. All in all, I was sent to at least ten different camps.

We were quite a bunch! My cousin Leah and I stayed together in some of the camps. We were lucky, usually they tried to scatter people so they weren't with people they knew from their villages or towns.

When we arrived at that first camp, we put our belongings on mattresses on the floor. They had told us to bring sheets and blankets, and clothes for several weeks. Six weeks was the longest amount of time I spent in a German camp. Between camps I attended a commercial school in Warsaw. I mainly took home study courses part-time, and only until 1942.

In the camps we did a lot of marching and singing. The women leaders – we called them *Führerinnen* – taught us songs to sing by memory. And then we marched. There were perhaps 100-150 girls my age, and all of us marched and sang. We sang Volkslieder and many Soldatenlieder such as *Muss i denn, Einmal am Rhein, Lustig ist das Zigeunerleben, Der Mai ist gekommen, Lili Marleen,* and so on.

There were different types of girls from all over in those camps. Many were from East Prussia, from up north near Königsberg (today, Kaliningrad). We thought they were the brave ones! They were much more German than we were. They spoke High German, and their ways were closer to the German ways.

Those girls may have found out where we were from by our accents. They stuck together a bit more. They were of a higher class than we were, and they seemed very smart. When the teacher taught us things, those girls would think it was nothing. They already knew the answers. I guess they had grown up in a German territory, so they had learned quite a bit of the material in school.

It also seemed to me that these Prussian girls loved the camps. For them it was a real *Erholung.* But for us it was hard, and we looked forward to the end. I don't remember the teachers treating us differently. But it was obvious that we were different. They dressed fancier and seemed more energetic, or more "with it" than we were. We were plainer, and we were farm people. They mostly came from cities and towns. They did not treat us badly, but we could just sense a different attitude. As a kid, I was pretty sensitive to different attitudes. Now it is okay with me that people are different. If you are that way, that is fine. But I am happy being the way I am.

They separated us into age groups. I was in the group of 14-18 year-olds, and then there was another group of 18 and older. We stayed in the camps day and night, for a period of three to six weeks. The boys were taken to different camps. They called the girls "BDM" or *"Bund Deutscher Mädel"* ("League of German Girls") and the boys were in *"Arbeitsdienst"* ("work-service"). I think the boys had to work a little harder than we did.

There were cooks and helpers who lived in the camps too. They cooked for all of us. We ate our food at long tables. We thought that was pretty nice. In the mornings the *Führerinnen* woke us up with music, then we washed ourselves. They taught us to keep ourselves very clean, with our hair washed and neatly combed. After our cold-water showers, we would march for an hour or so, and then we would have breakfast – kind of like soldiers.

It's a good thing there were only girls in that camp because we took our showers outside! That was so strange to me. At home we did our bathing inside the kitchen in the winter. In the summer we had an outside kitchen where we heated our water in big kettles. We had shutters on our windows which we closed when we bathed.

We were glad we had those shutters during the war. Otherwise we would have needed to hang blankets over the windows each night to keep the light from escaping. The government issued strict orders to keep all light from escaping through windows and doors. This was to prevent airplanes overhead from seeing where to bomb in the night. We used those shutters at night, but we wanted to be careful anyway, so we just used one small lantern in the evenings. Often we sat together and talked a little bit, or ate apples and went to bed before too late.

The Germans fed us good food in the camps. We never had large portions, but we had enough. I remember that there wasn't much to eat at home since the war had begun. But at the camps they fed us very well. I think that was supposed to make us want to keep going back to the camps.

Each day before we ate, we folded our hands and said, "Guten Appetit!" or "Wir haben Hunger!" ("We are hungry!"). We would say it in a normal voice, but the *Führerinnen* would yell, "It's not loud enough! Louder!" So we would yell louder.

After breakfast, we lined up outside and marched two by two and sang. The Führerinnen taught us the songs and accompanied us on the accordion. We learned the words from the blackboard, and then we repeated the songs over and over again till we had them memorized. Those songs are still in my head. I think that was their way of teaching us German, and the ways of the Nazis.

In the camps we also learned how to salute with our feet together and with our arms held out in front of us, crying out, "Heil Hitler!" Sometimes they told us we were holding our arms too high, sometimes too low. They had to be just right. We always had to greet one another that way. My cousin and I thought it so funny that we should have to say that whenever we greeted anyone.

In the afternoons we were supposed to take a nap. After that, we read all kinds of books out loud: books about the history of

Germany, or the government. Most of it went over our heads, but we listened anyway.

When we arrived at the first camp, we were given uniforms to wear. They made us look like little soldiers. The uniform was a navy skirt, a white blouse, a tie with a leather knot, and a jacket with a swastika on the arm. I thought, "Oh dear, I am a Nazi already!" We had to wear the uniform everyday in the camps. When we went home the teachers said, "Just keep it on, go home like this, show them what you are and that the Germans are teaching you good things." But I thought I would do it my way. So I always put the uniform in a suitcase and put on my civilian clothes for the trip home.

My Mom told me that we should try to be good to the Polish people, so we wouldn't make enemies. I didn't want to show off or try to be different from my Polish friends and neighbors, so I hid my uniform when I came home. But there were girls who showed off their German uniforms. They were so proud!

Each time I returned home from the Nazi camps, my parents wanted to know what had happened and what they had taught us. They were worried. But they knew that other children had to go to the camps too, and they said that while Germany was in power, we had to do what we were told.

When I told them that we were supposed to learn that Hitler was God now, their faces became sad. Dad said that this was wrong. He told me that I should stay strong and keep believing in the Lord. "Remember what we have taught you," he said. That was not a problem for me. I thought I would never give up my faith or really follow in the true Nazi way. I followed on the outside, I did what the others did, but I did not believe on the inside.

Something indeed was missing in the *Bund*. Church was missing. And if we were living without church, where were we going? In my home I had been brought up to believe that "six days you are to work, and the seventh day you are to rest." This was more than a tradition, it was a kind of *Ordnung*, or pattern for living – going to church and worshipping, and calling it the Lord's Day. Even now sometimes when we are sick, or in winter when the weather is so cold and we don't go to church, I feel that something is missing.

In those camps there was nothing different about Sunday. On Sunday we marched and sang as usual, shouting out "Heil Hitler."

Then is when I would often cry. I was so lonesome for home, and I was determined they would not take from me my Mennonite style of living. When I was 16 my grandmother gave me a New Testament. I took it along to the various Bund camps, and I would read, especially the Gospels. This helped me to keep safe, deep within me, the tradition of my childhood. Each time I read I would fold my hands, and the other *Bund* girls would laugh at me. So I finally stopped doing this and put the New Testament away. Yet I still had so much from my parents which I wanted to keep in my heart. I prayed by myself, quietly, and tried not to do some of the things some other girls were doing or saying, and hoped the two or three weeks in camp would be over soon so that I could return home. I said to myself, "Even if I must die, I want to follow the Lord."

My Mom knew what would happen to me in those camps if I refused to say "Heil Hitler." So she simply said: "Say it in the German camps if you have to, but don't say it otherwise."

My parents wondered what would happen in the war. They did not like what the Germans were doing in Poland, but they were scared of the Russians too. They heard that the Communists were taking people captive to work in concentration camps in Siberia. Dad said that one side will win and one will lose, that in all wars it turns out that way; but if Hitler won it would just be communism number two. People were tired of the fighting already and saw no hope either way.

As I have already mentioned, in 1941 and 42 many men from our village and surrounding areas were forced into the German military and were fighting on the Russian front. Most of our men were killed in these battles. Some families had a father and two or three sons fighting in Russia, and sometimes they all would be killed. It seemed that every day the postal services would bring a letter saying that someone from the village had been killed. I thought, they have to come back when the war is over. But I slowly realized, they would not come back.

My brother Edmund went to fight Russia too. By then he was 21. Emma and I were working in the field when we heard the news that he had been killed. They sent us his wallet with some pictures and a few letters, everything was spattered with his blood. I threw down my rake and cried out. I sobbed and sobbed. I could not believe that he was dead. Emma said to me later, "I think your heart was broken that day for the first time in your life."

During this time the stores were empty, and Dad said, "If the war does not end soon, all of us will be very poor. We will no longer have clothes on our backs or food to eat." My Dad believed that people should live in peace. When the Jews were taken to concentration camps, my father felt what was happening was unthinkable. Dad felt that it was wrong to teach us that Hitler was a God. But he also said we needed to fear the Communists. They are constantly taking people to work in concentration camps in Siberia. Everybody was tense, we all lived with fear, and it was pretty hard to cope.

Throughout the German occupation we teenage girls were forced to travel to and from the BDM camps, usually by train, but sometimes by bus. The trains and the tracks were often damaged during the war, but it didn't take them long to fix them, and soon the trains were rolling like in normal times. The second BDM camp I went to was in Modlin, just across the river. At that camp all we did was learn to cook with very few rations. The idea was that we should learn to be resourceful so that Germany could win the war.

At Modlin there was a big building complex. Dad said in the First World War the Russians used it to store ammunition, since it was in central Poland. During the Second War it became the biggest hospital in the area for the soldiers. In between our cooking lessons we had to go to that hospital and feed the soldiers. The Red Cross trains brought the wounded from the Russian front. Since the tracks were down a little hill, we could sit on the hill and look in the windows of the trains and see the soldiers lying there with blood seeping through their bandages. That was in 1941 or 42, and the fighting was very heavy.

When we saw those wounded soldiers we knew that the war was coming closer to us, and the fighting was getting worse. There were not enough nurses, so we girls would help feed the soldiers. We took them the cakes we had baked in the camp. I think they wanted to have us girls feed them to help make them feel better. We were supposed to serve them cake and talk to them – tell them our names and what we were doing. Some of them were so injured they could hardly talk. But some would ask us questions and talk with us. I was maybe 15 or 16 years old and I was quite shy. During the breaks Leah and I would go into the washroom and hide! We felt sorry for the soldiers and we wanted to help, but we weren't ready for entertaining boys! The matron at the camp pushed us to do it. She said we should keep them company so they wouldn't be so lonely.

I remember it was so sad to see such young boys all cut up and injured. Some of them were just lying there for weeks and weeks. Many of them had frozen fingers and toes from fighting in Russia. Perhaps they weren't as badly injured as the others, but they had to wait until their fingers and toes healed before they could go back to the front.

The next camp was in Litzmanstadt. This one was a little different from the others. They taught us in the evening in what they called *Abendschule*, or evening school. Since our writing was not very good, they showed us how to write neatly. The teacher wrote poems on the blackboard, and we had to copy them into our books. She said we should learn them by memory. I memorized the short ones, but the German words were so big that the longer ones were hard for me to remember. We had to stand up in front of the class and either read or recite the poems.

I was with my cousin Leah in that camp too. But after that, they started mixing us up. The next camp I was in was near Königsberg. In addition to the marching, singing and the lectures, they took us out to the fields to help bring in the potato harvest. Many of the farmers were fighting in the war and they needed all the extra hands they could find to help bring in the harvest.

The scariest time for me came when I was sent to a camp in Potsdam, near Berlin. The Allies were bombing Berlin, and the fighting was really heavy. We went to that camp on the train, but as we got close to Berlin the tracks were damaged and the trains had to stop. In many a city along the way this had happened, where all the buildings, still in flame and smoke, were reduced to rubble. They used prisoners – French and Polish people, and people from Czechoslovakia – to clear and repair the tracks quickly. At Potsdam we often heard the phrase, "Räder müssen rollen für den Sieg" ("The wheels must continue rolling for victory"), and the box cars above those wheels needed to be filled. This is where we young girls also fit in: we had been brought in to do our share in helping to win the war.

When we arrived in Potsdam they took us to bunkers far beneath the ground. There were big warehouses beneath the ground too. We took an elevator to reach the bunkers. In that camp there weren't very many of us: maybe only 50 or 75.

In that camp we assembled packages. At first we didn't know what they were for, but then the *Führerinnen* told us that they were Christmas packages for the soldiers. It was funny to me that they didn't believe in God, but when Christmas time came, they arranged for the soldiers to receive gifts. Christmas itself wasn't a special day at all, though.

We packed a pair of gloves, some packages of cigarettes, a nice chunk of chocolate and sometimes some crackers. They called them *zwei Kilo* packets. Sometimes we put socks in the packages, and sometimes we put in meat, or pork and beans. There were mounds and mounds of the gloves and chocolate and the rest, and we just put the packages together and bundled them up.

We slept on bunk beds down in that bunker. I think they had brought girls there before to do the same thing. We stayed beneath the ground the whole time we were there. After a while the hours started to feel really long. I always like to be outside, so being in that camp was really hard for me. It was also very frightening. We could hear the bombs falling outside, and we didn't know what would happen to us. I remember thinking, "Why should I have to go to Germany to be killed?" In my village it was quiet. But the big cities were getting bombed.

When we were finished with our work, we came up from the bunker to the light. I remember that we couldn't leave right away because the train station had been totally destroyed. But in a couple of hours the trains were rolling again. The Germans were very organized that way. Their number one priority was to keep the transportation lines open.

After the camp in Potsdam, we went to a camp in Sochaczew. At Sochaczew we had to learn a lot. We did a lot of marching and singing and shouting. One of our teachers there loved art so much, so we created a lot of art and we also performed drama. I made a few friends in the camps, but none who were very close. We didn't write letters when it was over or anything. I must say I did not care too much. I was just glad when it was over.

From Sochaczew we went to Płock. I remember Mom and Dad saying that it was hard each time to let me go. I was needed on the farm too, to help pick fruit and do other work. But the Germans told us that it would only be for a short time.

After the camp in Płock, I came home and said I was not going back anymore. So when the orders came for me to go to another camp, I just didn't go. Pretty soon they found out that we had disobeyed orders, and there were policemen on our yard, talking to Dad. They said, "You have a choice: you can either go to jail for a while, or you can pay 50 Deutschmarks." I don't know how long Dad would have had to stay in jail, but he didn't want to go at all. So he paid them the 50 marks. That time I didn't have to go. But soon more orders came in the mail, and again I had to go.

Eventually I turned 18 and was old enough to get a job and stop going to the camps. I was lucky to get a job at the government flour mill just across the river, close to our house. Leah's older sister worked as a secretary at that mill, but she was expecting a baby. Since she had to stop working to have her baby, we arranged for me to take over her job. I was a little bit afraid, since I didn't know much about working in an office. So she said she would teach me how to do everything – bookkeeping, buying grains from the local farmers, and the other office work.

When my cousin worked there, she lived with an older Polish couple just one house away from the mill. When I came to learn from her, I slept on a couch in her room. The Polish lady was very nice to us. She cooked for both of us. I had ration cards which allowed me to get a little more meat and bread. And while I worked at the mill, my boss said when I needed some extra flour I should take some. So I would ask for a little more every now and then, and I would take it home to that Polish family, and the woman used it to make bread.

After two weeks, my cousin moved out and I took over. I was there for another eight months. On weekdays I stayed at the Polish family's house, but I spent most of my weekends at home. The government gave me a bike to use to get around, since I was working for them. It was such a nice bike!

I was paid a little money at that job. Not too much, but enough to cover my room and board, and to have a little extra left over.

There was not much to buy, though. Everything was rationed, even clothes. We got a pair of shoes each year and those of us who were working for the government got a little bit extra. When they saw that we needed a coat or a jacket we would get a little more on top of our rations.

I really enjoyed my job at the mill, which was across the river and about ten kilometers towards Płock from my home. It was surrounded by Polish farms. The farmers had to produce a certain amount of grain, depending on how big the farm was, and deliver it to our mill. There was a lot of paperwork involved.

I worked with a lot of Polish people in the mill. They were really nice. We usually spoke to each other in Polish, but when the Germans came around, I spoke only German. I found out that the SS was in charge of the mill. It sat very close to the river, and boats came from Warsaw or from Płock to deliver grain and pick up flour. There was a bakery in a town nearby, and from time to time they came and gave us fresh-baked bread.

In front of the mill there was a big scales where we weighed the wheat. One of the Polish workers was in charge of the scales. He weighed the bags of grain as they came in. He would come into the office where there was a door with a window in it, and he would slip me the ticket with the name of the farmer and the amount of grain. Then I paid the farmer his money. I also had to help keep track of the flour that was milled. When we filled an order of flour, we loaded the boat and the buyers paid us for it.

There were twenty of us workers at the mill. The rest were all men, and they were all Polish. In those years I knew them all by name. The miller was a very nice gentleman. Later on, after the war I realized that there were some Polish people who were very hard and brutal, as if they didn't even have a heart. But at the mill I knew many who were very nice to me.

I didn't mind being the only girl at the mill. I didn't work very closely with the others. I did my work in the office, and they came and went and did their work. There were different shifts, since the mill was running day and night. But my hours were nine o'clock until 4:30 in the afternoon.

In the evenings after work I went back to the house where I stayed. There was no radio, no papers, no telephone, no letters to write. Often I sat with a book and read, or I knitted or crocheted. I would make a pair of gloves or a sweater, or go for a walk and sit by the river. I ate my meals with the Polish couple. It was kind of a lonely time, but my work gave me enough to keep me occupied and satisfied most of the time.

When I had enough money saved, I took a day off and went to Płock to buy material for a winter dress. The stores in Płock were owned by Germans – the Poles didn't have stores there anymore. There were some shoe stores and fabric stores, but they didn't have very much to sell. But I found some fabric for my dress. That was just before the end of the war.

The Russians came through in February of 1945. Mom and Dad were on the farm, and I was still working at the mill. On the radio we started to hear that the German front wasn't holding anymore. The Russians were pushing forward. We also were told that if the Russians took Warsaw, it would be easy for them to push farther West. I think the Germans and the Russians were pushing one another back and forth quite a bit during this time span of four weeks or so. Some days the front was very close, and we could hear the cannons like thunder. Other days it was quiet, since the front was farther away to the East.

During this time we as a family decided to flee. We packed blankets, warm clothing and food into our wagon, and started out, but found it far too dangerous to continue. Retreating German tanks and trucks, and horse-drawn wagons filled the roads and were constantly being bombed and strafed with machine gun fire. So we returned home.

One day there was a huge explosion on the river. Usually when the bombs fell, they came from airplanes overhead. But this time there was no airplane, no sound to warn us. The source of the bomb must have been 20 or 30 kilometers to the East. Indeed, the Russians by now were using new and powerful, long-range weapons. All of a sudden, one of the boats carrying the flour blew up. Everybody immediately dropped to the floor to keep out of the way of the flying glass and wood. We had been trained to drop to the floor when bombs fell. I don't think anyone was seriously hurt in that explosion.

One day soon after that explosion, I arrived at the mill and everybody was packing and getting ready to flee before the Russians

came. There was a German SS man in charge who lived with his wife
and two daughters in a little house just up the hill from the mill.
They were packing a big wagon with all their things, and when he
found out I wanted to go home to my parents he said to me, "Edna,
don't go back." My home was toward the front, and he invited me
to come with them in their wagon. But I said no. I knew them very
well, and I trusted them, but I wanted to find my parents.

In fact, many Polish workers in the mill were also telling me,
"Don't go back, you will go across the river, and the Russians are so
close they might catch you on the way home."

But I replied, "Whatever happens to my parents will happen
to me."

Then the SS man reminded me, "They do things to the girls
and to the mothers!"

And I thought, I would rather be shot or stabbed to death
than be raped. Oh, I was so terrified! Throughout the war and after
the war we saw so many young girls with babies, older women with
babies. Horrible! This was the hardest for me to see.

I was so scared. Inside I was filled with terror, and I was
preparing to die. I knew that when the Russians came they might kill
us right away. But I wanted to be with my parents. So I rode home
on my bike as fast as I could.

On the way I passed a lot of German soldiers in trenches who
were watching the skies for airplanes. "Where are you going?" they
asked. Perhaps they thought I was a spy, but I just told them I was
going home. There were soldiers everywhere, and many were so
young! They were just children. Some of the soldiers were looking
at pictures they carried with them, and many were crying. It was so
sad. The Russians were closing in, and to me it seemed like the end
of the world.

There was a bridge very close to our house. Before the German
occupation we used a ferry to cross the river, but the Germans built
a temporary pontoon bridge during the war. I was part way across
this bridge when I heard a soldier on the other side whistling at me.

He was sitting on a motorbike and singing a song, "Erika,
Erika," which was a popular song for little girls. "Kleine Erika, where
are you going?" I thought he was just teasing me, so I pedaled faster.

I was all by myself on that bridge. Then, just when I reached the other side of the bridge, the whole thing exploded behind me!

Wood and dirt flew everywhere, and there was a big cloud of black smoke. I threw my bike down and ran, and jumped into a trench with the soldiers. Everything was flying around us. The dirt nearly covered us, and the smoke was thick and black.

The Germans had put explosives underneath, so it would take the Russians longer to cross the river. I guess that soldier was trying to warn me.

Miraculously, nobody was badly injured. We could have been killed by the flying sticks and dirt, but most of us had little more than scratches. There was so much dirt on my back, however, that I couldn't even move, and some soldiers had to help dig me out.

Since I was so close to home, I wanted to run and try to reach my parents. The soldiers helped me shake off the mud and sticks that had fallen on top of us. I never saw my nice bike again. I think I left it there by that trench.

I ran as fast as I could run to our farm. There were trucks full of German soldiers all over our garden and the gardens next door. There were tanks and trucks all over the place. Some of the military trucks had girls in them too. Many of the German soldiers who were in the cities had girls that they took with them when they retreated. I saw one girl sitting in the back of a truck, eating a piece of chocolate. I wondered, "What is she doing there?" But I guess she wanted to be safe too. People certainly did things differently during the war.

When I got home Mom and Dad were so pale and scared! We were all very frightened about what would happen when the Russians came in. Would they kill us immediately? Send us to Siberia? Imprison us? The Germans were running everywhere, and destroying everything they could before the Russians came. There was shooting everywhere, and the sky turned red from the smoke and the spotlights. Warsaw was aflame and we could see it from home. Cannon shells flew – one hit our house, creating a gaping hole. We were in the midst of battle, and I thought, this is the end.

We again considered fleeing. But this time it was too late. Many who were fleeing were simply cut down, left and right, by the bullets and bombs of the Russian planes. It seemed safer to remain in our home.

Dad said, "We don't know what will happen, but the main thing is, we will meet in heaven. Right now, we should prepare our hearts to be ready for heaven."

We had that night together. Dad prayed and read the Bible. We held each others' hands, and Mom said, "It cannot go farther than the end." Somehow, we were prepared to die.

Then there was no more talking, and my parents and I waited through the night. I was so tired, I no longer cared what would happen. We did not eat that day, we were so scared. I said to Mom, I'm just going to bed, what happens will happen. Mom and Dad stayed up, and I slept through the whole night. That night the Germans dug a hole next to our house and put a big cannon in it, in order to shoot across the river at the oncoming Russians.

By morning Dad and Mom still had not slept. The German cannon was gone, the Germans were gone, yet we could do nothing but wait. In the morning Dad told me and Mom to go upstairs and hide in the little room we used to smoke meat. He was afraid that when the Russians came they would try to rape us. I guess he knew that this happened quite often after a war. From inside the smoke room we could hear him walking around. The Russian soldiers came to our door and asked Dad where the Germans went. My Dad spoke Russian very well, so when he spoke to them, they didn't know he was a German, so they left.

By dinner time, three other men came – one Polish soldier and two civilians. We were in the kitchen, Mom was making some soup. They came and said that Dad had to go with them, they wanted to ask him a few questions. Dad turned around a little bit and looked sadly at Mom and me as they were pushing him out the door. And I remembered the other time he was taken away, when the war first broke out. I thought that maybe this time, too, he would come back.

From one yoke we had been saved, now we were entering another. Dad put his warm jacket on, and I ran back and brought him his shawl for around his neck and I hugged him. The Poles were kind of standing around and looking at us. Mom said later that perhaps they had planned to take us all, but they just took Dad. Once more I ran back and broke a piece of bread Mom had ready, and put it in Dad's pocket. And that was all we could do. I was 18 years old. I never saw my Dad again.

A CRUMBLING WORLD

My sister Emma and her two boys came to our house soon after they took Dad away. We were very frightened and we wondered what would happen to us. That afternoon, a group of Polish soldiers and civilians came to our house. There weren't any Russians in this group.

First they took our horses and the few cows we had in the barn. They chased the chickens, and killed one of our pigs right there in the yard. They stole whatever they wanted, and destroyed what they didn't want. They had brought a wagon with them. First they loaded the animals onto the wagon, and then they came into the house to load more things.

They took the best things first: the rings off Mom's hands, and watches. They loaded our furniture and dishes onto the wagon. When they left, we thought maybe that was all they would take. But the next day more people came and filled their bags with whatever they could find in the house – even the forks and knives. We just stood and watched them, shaking. They could have shot us, and that would have been the end.

Before the Russians came through, we had buried some of our things in holes in the yard. We buried our best china and the cream separator. We thought that when everything was quiet again, we would at least have something. But we lost it all. Mom told us not to worry. She had lived through the first war and had lost everything then too. But she had rebuilt her life. So she told us to keep quiet and let them take what they wanted to take. As long as they didn't hurt us, we would be all right.

One scene sticks in my mind so clearly. The Polish plunderers came into our house cursing and yelling. They ran through all the rooms and opened all the doors, breaking everything they could. Then one of them saw our German Bible on the cupboard in the kitchen. "Look, here is a Hitler book," he said. Laughing, they ripped it apart and used the pages in the Bible to roll their cigarettes. They gave everybody a puff and smoked right there in our house, just to show us what power they had.

Then they looked at us and said, "You have nice clothes on. Our children are much poorer than yours, they don't have any clothes." And they started taking our clothes from us. My sister was there with her two boys, and they even took the little coat from the older boy, and his shoes. We had put on our older clothing, but they took it anyway. They were yelling, "Give me this, we need that," and, "you will see what it means to be poor and have nothing." They took my sweater too, and two dresses.

"Now we need workers," they said, "to clean up the mess that the Germans left." They looked at Emma with her two children, and I think they were a little softer with her. But they looked at me and said "Come, we need to clean the fire station." So they took me from the yard with a gun pointed at my back. I couldn't even say good-bye to Mom and Emma. Not even one word.

They marched me to a place where they had gathered 30 or 40 people already. The group was mostly older women and girls from the surrounding villages. Many of the people with German ancestry had fled to Germany before the Russians arrived. Those of us who were left were rounded up and forced to work. They did not ask us where we came from, or if we were Polish, but only asked for our names. To me they said, "Oh, with a name like that, you are certainly German."

It made them very happy to taunt us; they were doing a good job, catching and arresting all those Germans and bringing them together. Most of us were women and children, there were very few men. Most of the men had been killed on the Russian front, or on their way home when they were chased out of Russia. By 1945, there were very few men left.

The soldiers made us walk seven kilometers to Leoncin where they made us clean horse manure from the old fire station on the town square. During the occupation the Germans had used the building as a stable for their horses and it was filled with dirt and manure.

Next to the fire station, on the same side of the square, there was a Catholic church. On the side next to it there was a big government building which the Germans had built as barracks for the police and the soldiers who guarded the border with Warsaw. The building also housed a prison in the basement, where until 1945 the Germans imprisoned those Poles whom they had arrested. Now that the Germans were gone, the Poles arrested us and put us in this prison, saying, "Now you can taste what we went through for five years." They packed us in at night – 30, 40, as many as 70 – into a few small rooms where we slept on the floor on a little lice-filled straw, sometimes not even straw. We had no water for bathing, no toilets. And men and women were kept together.

On another side of the square there was a small open space with a flagpole. Every morning they raised the Polish flag on that pole. And on the fourth side of the square there was an office building. There was also a road into the square. We had to load the manure from the firehouse onto the wagons and drag it outside the square on that road. We had no shovels, and we had no horses, so we loaded the wagons by hand and pulled them by hand. A few people would hold onto the wagon by the posts which stuck out from the front, where the horses would have been attached, and a few would grab the back end. We pushed and pulled that full wagon until we could get it moving along the road. We pulled it all the way outside town and dumped it there.

Then they brought us pails with water, and brushes made from willow sticks, and we swept out each of the rooms in the fire house. When we were finished with that, they chased us back into the basement of the big building where the German police had been. The Polish police had already set up their offices there. Each night we slept in that basement and in the morning they chased us out to work.

The Polish people threw the biggest party to celebrate their victory! They were so happy that the war was over, and that they had some German prisoners. When we had finished cleaning out the old fire station, we heard music in the town square. They took us out of the basement and into the square and treated us so roughly! Sometimes I can still hear that awful music that they played.

Our second job at the Leoncin prison was to close the trenches. The Germans had dug trenches all over, and when the Poles took us prisoner, we had to fill in the trenches. The Poles said, "You Germans, you dug up our Polish ground, and now it is your job to fill up and level our land again." There were close to 70 of us, women and children, and we shoveled the ground with our hands till the trenches were closed. That's what we did, day after day. It was horrible what they made us do. If we had had spades or other tools, it would have been easier, but they made us do this with our bare hands. They put us all in a row. The trenches were some six feet deep, and they kept us to this until all the trenches in the area were leveled.

This was the hardest time for me. Leoncin was close to home, so many people knew me from before the war. That made it very difficult. Also, this was the smallest group of prisoners I was in and they made us do whatever they wanted. There was no real government yet, just the wild people who were crazy with victory and the end of the war. There was no structure, no organization. People could do whatever they wanted with you, and it seemed there was no law. For the first few months, it was chaos.

Usually it was Polish civilians who came and ordered us around. Sometimes they had a soldier with them, but sometimes they just said, "We won the war, so now you have to do what we tell you to do." They wanted to do to us what the Germans had done to them. And it was true, they had been badly mistreated by the Germans. I thought about the German Amtskommisar, who was the commander of our area. He was so mean; he kicked Polish people off their farms and sent others away to work somewhere. I felt that they should find *him* and make *him* clean up the fire station and fill those trenches, not us!

I found out that the Poles had formed two political parties. One was the PPR and one was the UBP. I forget now what the letters mean, but one was the Labor party and one was the Communist party. They were fighting over who would take control of the government. There had been fighting on the front, and now, fighting behind the front. The civilians, again caught in the fray, had to suffer much. Eventually the Russians gained control of the whole area. Many of the Poles who were in power for a time were from the lower classes. Some of them couldn't even write their names, but they were trying to run the government!

After a few weeks in Leoncin, they shaved our heads. They did that so that we couldn't run away. If we tried to run, someone would recognize that we were prisoners by our shaved heads. I think it looks funny when a man has a shaved head, but it is much worse to see women with no hair! Sometimes when we were in the forest, chopping wood, we would find scraps of clothing on the ground. I remember that we picked up scraps and wrapped them around our heads to hide our baldness.

We also wore the clothes we found on the ground. We only had the clothing that we were wearing when they captured us, and it was getting so ragged and worn. So we used whatever we could find. One woman found a skirt and she gave it to me to wear, but it was very torn. So we took a piece of wire and wrapped it around the waist to hold it together.

Life at this time was so hard. I didn't think I was going to make it through. For the first three or four days we were given nothing to eat, and they beat us and terrorized us all the time. Oh, they tortured us! The blood was just running. They did horrible things! In the prison, they would crash us into the windows and sometimes the broken glass would fly out of the frames. I remember thinking, "Why don't they just shoot me? Then it will go no farther than this – it will all be over."

There were many offices in the building, and in every office a soldier with a rubber whip and pistol. They would even shoot people in those offices. We then had to drag off the bodies and clean up the mess.

One day they led me through the kitchen to an office. There was an officer in there, behind a desk. He started asking me questions. And I remember I stood in a corner, pushing my back against the wall, trying to hide somehow. But he walked over to me and began beating me in the face; first one side and then the other side, again and again. The next few days my face was black and blue and very swollen. It was so horrible!

They asked us all kinds of questions, trying to get us to say that we supported Hitler. They wanted to know if I had been a Nazi, and if I had worked for the government. Luckily, when I was at the mill and the Russians were coming, I had burned everything that showed I had been in the Hitler camps and had worked for the government. I knew it would be bad if anyone found out I had been in those BDM camps. I burned my uniform, and now I realized it was a good thing that I had never worn it when I came home from the German youth camps.

When they asked me questions, I knew my future was going to be dark anyway, so I thought the best thing to do was to lie and tell them that I had never been in a Nazi camp. They said that if I didn't tell them they would shoot me, but I knew that if I told them I had been in the Nazi camps they would shoot me anyway. So I lied. Oh, I think that was my first lie in my life! For a long time my heart was very heavy with these things I had to do. Now I know that the Lord has forgiven me.

They took us into an office one at a time, and they would beat us with their rifle butts for a while, and then they would chase us back to the basement again and leave us alone. But before too long, they would wake us up again and start the questions all over again. They thought that if we were sleepy we would be a little confused and would tell them the truth. But I knew that they could beat me all they wanted to, I would never tell them that I had been in those camps.

I remember vividly a mother who in ten years of marriage had borne no children, but who gave birth in wartime. She too was called into one of the torture offices and accused of being a member of Hitler's party. She had this little baby wrapped in some rags, and they ripped that baby out of her arms, and threw it into the corner. Then they beat that woman up until she could not walk. She was covered with blood from top to bottom. I never saw that mother or child again.

One of the worst things I can remember was watching them beat some older men they had caught. They made them lie face down on a bench and they beat them so badly with rubber whips that their blood gushed onto the floor. And their clothes were soaked from the blood.

When they finished beating them, they called us in and we had to clean up the blood with a pail of water. Those poor men! I can still hear in my ears the way those men yelled. It wasn't with a normal voice. They killed a few people that way. They beat us up too. They beat me with a rubber whip. I was black and blue everywhere, and I passed out. They threw me into the basement and then splashed a pail of cold water on me to make me come to.

One time they kicked me down and beat me so badly that my skin was terribly cut up. I couldn't walk for several days after that, I could only lie on the floor. There were no bandages, and no water for washing. That's the way they treated us in that first camp.

They didn't allow us to speak German after the war. We could only speak Polish or Russian. One day we were out in the forest gathering wood when we passed an old woman. I said to her, "Guten Morgen!" I was beaten so badly for this. The officers threw me down and beat me with a rubber whip on my back and the back of my legs and said, "The next time you speak that Hitler language, we'll kill you and cut you into pieces like a herring!" And so I learned to remain quiet. War and its aftermath teach you to be quiet. I found out that saying even half a word was sometimes exactly the wrong thing to do. Sometimes I even thought I had lost my ability to express myself in words.

In time my wounds and bruises healed. However, one of my kidneys was permanently damaged due to the many beatings. And for years I dreaded looking at my back in the mirror.

One reason they didn't kill more of us was that they needed us to work, especially for gathering wood. They ordered us to cut wood in the forest and load it onto the train which would transport it to Russia for heating. The Poles were angry. Oh, they were angry! They said, "We do not have enough wood either, and what the Germans did not ruin, now the Russians will take." And the Russians did take wood, and lots of other stuff. They took us out to the forest each day, early in the morning. We sawed wood with our hand-saws and stacked it into piles. When we cut and stacked enough, we loaded it onto trains. Then in the evening, the soldiers took us back to our prison.

The basement where we were kept used to be the bakery for the government office. They kept all of us German women and the Poles who had cooperated with the Germans down there. The basement had a big iron door that was fastened with a heavy nail. For many years afterwards I could still hear the sound of that door in my ears. In the mornings at five o'clock a Polish man would open the door and yell at us, "Come and work, that's enough sleeping here!"

One day one of the women didn't move when the man yelled at us. I think her name was Mrs. Klein. She was a Baptist, and had twin girls who were 15 or 16 years old. And she just could not take it. She could not stand to see what they did to her and her girls, so during that night she had hanged herself on the hook on the window. When the policeman came into the room in the morning to wake us up, she didn't move. She was lying on the floor, covered up. He gave her a good kick. But she was already dead and we didn't even know it.

One of the most difficult things for me was to watch how the Poles treated the local young men who had been forced to become soldiers for Germany. Some of them had been captured, others had run away and made their way back to their villages to find their families. Many were caught by the Polish police and brought to the camp. Often these men were killed. They were tortured so much that they just died.

I remember watching them beat two young men I had known from school. One was from a Müller family, and he was my age. The Poles took them out and beat them up. They made them move a hay machine – one pulled and the other pushed. And while they were trying to move this huge piece of farm machinery, the drunken Poles were beating them and beating them the whole time. When the Poles got tired of beating them, they left the young men lying in the road, half-dead.

After they died, three or four of us women were taken from the basement and forced to bury them. The Poles said, "bury them like the dogs they were." It was a Sunday. We dragged them from the road, and since we couldn't bury them in the cemetery, we dug into the sand by the woods with our hands. All we could do was make a shallow hole and cover them with a bit of sand. A few days later, when they again chased us into the forest to saw wood, as we passed by the graves, we saw that dogs had found the bodies – it was so awful!

One day, one of the Polish officers called me out of the group. I wondered, "Oh, what will happen now? This is my end. He will rape me, or kill me, or both," I thought. He led me to a place in the basement, near where we were kept for the night. There were steps going down into a square hole which may have held a furnace at one time. He handed me two pails and told me to fill the hole with water from the well nearby. I brought water, bucket by bucket, until the hole was nearly full. Then he told me, "Go stand in the hole until you die like a dog." So I went in. The water came up to my neck. I stood in that water the rest of that day, all night and the next day. I was so cold and so tired and it was very dark in that hole. I thought I would faint, and then drown. All around me I could hear shooting and running.

Finally, when I thought I couldn't stand it anymore, a different soldier came and told me I could come out of the hole. Later I found out what had happened to the officer who had put me in there. When the Germans were in power, many Poles chose to take German citizenship rather than be a prisoner. That is what this officer had done. He spoke many languages and could pass for different nationalities. We called him "Smart Fox". He had worked for the Germans in the concentration camps. He was just like a German.

When the Germans were driven out of Poland he ran away and pretended to be a Pole again. But he got caught. There were two widows who came to Leoncin to live after the war. They still had a cow, and were using it for milk and butter. The officer found out about their cow, and he took it away from them. That night the Poles had a big feast in the old firehouse, and killed and ate the cow. But the two women recognized the officer from when the Germans were in power, and they turned him in. The other Poles found that officer's papers and sent him away, probably to jail somewhere.

After Smart Fox left, and once the government became more settled, things became a bit better for us. I think the hatred cooled off somewhat after those first few weeks. They got most of their anger out, and they didn't treat us as badly after that. Life was still hard, but slowly it got better. They realized they couldn't treat us too badly, because they needed us to work.

Soon the Polish farmers needed us to help them in their fields. They would buy us for a bottle of whiskey and we would go work on their farms, helping with the planting or the harvest, cleaning houses, scrubbing walls. We'd work for a farmer for a while, and then he'd send us back to the basement prison. Some of the farmers were not very mean, but others yelled at us and called us names. They said, "It serves you right, you are just getting what we had to suffer during the war."

The Poles treated us the worst. I talked with other girls later who said that the Russians did not beat them. They gave them bread and slept with them, but they didn't beat them. Later, when I talked with the Dyck girls from West Prussia, they said that the Poles there beat them and tortured them and let them freeze. It was much the same for me.

All the time at these camps, we never knew what was coming. Sometimes at night they would wake us up and the policemen would be on horses or bicycles, and they would chase us maybe 30 or 40 kilometers through the night, through the forest to another camp. Sometimes prisoners would be given a spade, told to dig a hole, and then find out they had dug their own grave. Once a guard told two of us to dig such a hole, and I was sure he would then shoot us. I thought, "This is my last day; I will dig the hole, he will shoot me, and I will fall into the hole!" Fortunately for me, the guard actually wanted to see what was in the ground at that spot, and I could continue living in my fear.

One time I know they put a group of prisoners together and told them they were going to Warsaw. Instead, they sent them to Siberia. That was how some of the Poles would talk to us: "You are going to Siberia to die there; we don't want you to eat our bread here in Poland." This is the *Hass*, or hatred, that all wars create, on all sides. What people can stoop to in their hatred!

I was in that first prison camp in Leoncin for over a year, from February 1945 to the late winter of 46. After a while they gave us soup in the morning – potatoes and cabbage, and a kind of coffee. We thought that was pretty good. But we were always so hungry! It was so hard for me to see the hungry children crying. Perhaps their fathers were killed in the war, and their mothers were so hungry. There was nothing to do for them because there was so little food.

I often thought about how life was during the war, when there was all the shooting and bombing. Things were scary then, but I think the heaviest, most difficult part was after the war when we were prisoners. We lost all our rights and we were nothing, like rags. That's a German saying – "Wir sind lauter alte Lumpen" ("We are nothing but old rags"). And every day was filled with hunger and fear and humiliation.

I was so lonely, but at the same time I was thankful that I didn't have anyone depending on me. I thought about my Mom and my Dad, and my brothers and sister, and I missed them terribly. But when I saw the mothers with their children in the camps, so hungry and tired and cold, I was glad I didn't have anyone to take care of besides myself. At that time I thought I would never have children. I was so afraid of not being able to take care of them if another war were to come.

One day they came to us while we were still in the basement, and told us to go outside. Very often they would take people outside on the lawn, and just shoot them with their machine guns, or they loaded them up and sent them to Siberia. We heard about things like that happening. So we were all terribly frightened.

They sent us around the church on the corner and up the hill. They made us wait out there for most of the day, just standing. Nobody came and told us to leave or to go back to the village or to do anything. We wondered what would happen. Finally an officer came and said, "You know, we are very good to you. We could shoot you if we wanted. But we won't. Just go back to where you came from." So they sent us back to the basement. So again, I knew the Lord's hand was with me.

Even though so much had changed since the end of the war, there were still some people who were kind to us. I had known the priest and the cook at that Catholic church before the war. There was another lady there too, who helped clean the house. My Dad used to joke that she was the priest's wife. I thought that was funny. He had a cook, why did he need another woman in the house? This woman always looked so nice. We didn't see her very often, but we did see the cook.

The cook was such a nice lady! She was single, and had worked for the priest for many years. Like many Polish women, she had a shawl which she wore around her shoulders. When we were being kept in that basement, we weren't given very much food. But she came by our cells to sneak us some bread. She hid bits of bread under her shawl and pushed it through a broken windowpane to us as she walked by. Some of the windows in the basement were broken out, but she could not fit the whole loaf of bread through; she could only push bits of it through the holes in the broken window.

This was really a scary time. Every day we were so full of fear. And we usually didn't have much in our stomachs, but the fear made our stomachs turn so we would even throw up from the fear. But that cook came and gave us bread for our stomachs. We were desperately hungry, but when that bread came we split it into pieces so that everyone would have some. We organized and checked together so that everyone would have the same amount.

It was very dangerous for that cook to help us that way! The police came around very often, but she was very smart. She would go out for a walk with the bread under her shawl, and she would watch which way the policemen went. When they went around a corner or into another building, then she would go by our cell and drop the bread to us. We said that if she had not given us that bread we would have starved in the beginning. I really think that is true.

Some of the Polish people were very mean to us, but then some were so nice and went out of their way to treat us well. There were many Polish people who were good that way. But it seemed that the ones who were of a lower class, who could not even read and write, had taken control and were running things now. They were the ones who treated us poorly.

Sometimes I think that if the "normal" Poles had taken over when the Germans left and the war ended, things would have been much better. They would have said, "The war is over, now you do your thing and we'll do our thing." But the lower class Poles were so angry, and they took it out on us.

The Polish government and the police were housed in a building close to the church. They drank a lot and had parties in that building. Very often they would take me out of the basement and have me help in the kitchen, washing dishes or cooking for their parties. Then I had a chance to talk with the Priest's cook. Sometimes she would come to the kitchen when I was working there. I whispered thanks to her for bringing the bread, but she said, "I had to do it. A voice told me you were so hungry there and there was nobody to feed you."

One of the ladies I worked with in the kitchen was the wife of an officer. She was very friendly to me. One day she said that she and her husband were invited to a wedding, but their little boy had nothing to wear. We prisoners had almost nothing, but the Polish people were poor too. And there was nothing in the stores to buy, even if they did have money.

I suggested that maybe we could take apart wool from older sweaters and make a new one. The Poles had a big pile of clothes that they had taken off the German prisoners. So we sorted through that pile and found some yarn that would work.

With her permission, I knitted at night in the kitchen. We had no kerosene, but she told me to cut the wood for the stove a little thinner so I could keep the stove door open and knit by the light of the fire. We didn't have any knitting needles, so we took the spokes from a bicycle wheel and used them for needles. I think I knitted for a day and a half or so. I knitted into the night sitting by that fire, and finally that little sweater was finished. I was so happy that I didn't have to go back down in that cell to sleep, and she was happy to have that sweater.

While I was working on the sweater, the two parties started fighting again. We could hear running and shooting outside in the night. The officer's wife was in the next room, and she came to me and said, "Yrcka, we have to run." At that time everyone called me by a Polish name, since "Edna" was too German. She grabbed her little boy and the three of us jumped out her window and ran toward the Catholic cemetery, which was close by.

Soon after we got there, the shooting stopped. The Polish men were all beaten up and bloody from fighting, but we were still afraid that they would start again. The officer's wife said she would run to the priest's house to hide. I knew we couldn't go together, since she was Polish and I was German, and I was supposed to be in the basement. So I said I would stay in the cemetery and hide. I made a pile of wreaths and flowers where the graves were close together, and crawled under them and hid for the rest of the night. In the morning I crept to the priest's house where the officer's wife was, and the two of us made our way back to the house. By that time the men were all sleeping off their hangovers.

Later I worked for the wife of a different officer. My Dad knew her family pretty well. She had two miscarriages before and was now expecting her third baby. She wasn't feeling very well, and her husband came and got me from the camp to help take care of her. He knew that I spoke Polish pretty well, and so he asked me to look after his wife while he was at work.

They lived in a small house near the office building. The house was very dirty since she was sick in bed. So I thought I would make myself busy cleaning. I drew a pan of water and began to wash some clothes with soap and warm water.

I had only been there an hour or two, when all of sudden, the officer's wife started yelling. She was in terrible pain, and told me to call her husband. So I ran to him and told him that his wife was having trouble. We ran back to the house, and I stood there watching and wondering what would happen. There was only one room in the house, so I watched from behind a curtain that divided the room.

There was no doctor or nurse to help them. The baby was coming, and she was yelling at the top of her lungs. I had never seen anything like it in my life! The officer was a little bit drunk, I think, and he started yelling at me. When he was sober, he was quite a gentleman. But now he took out his pistol, and said he would shoot me right away. His wife looked at me and signaled for me to run. So I did. I thought, if I run, I'll probably be killed. But if I stay, I will be killed for sure. Better to take the chance on escaping.

I ran out to the outhouse, but that was too close, I thought. So I ran to a little barn which was farther away, and I stayed there with the goats and other animals until the officer cooled off. By morning things had quieted down, so I crept back into the house. By that time he was sober, and his wife had lost the baby. I kept working there for a few days, chopping wood and washing their clothes. She was still pretty sick, so she stayed in bed. He didn't threaten me again. I think he was a little ashamed, since he had known my Dad. But when he was drunk, he was just wild with anger.

I belonged to that officer for quite a while. After a month or so at Leoncin, most of the women had been "bought." When we were finished at one place and before someone else bought us, we came back to the camp at Leoncin and gathered wood. Sometimes there would be 30 of us at the camp, and sometimes just a few, depending on how many were out working on the farms.

On one farm they had me help them dig up potatoes. Many of the farmers had buried things in the ground during the war, to keep them safe and hidden from thieves. Some people hid potatoes this way. They dug big ditches and dumped the potatoes in them, and then they stacked wood on top of the ditches so people wouldn't think to dig underneath. First I had to throw the wood off and then dig up the ditch and get the potatoes out. Some of them were rotten, but some were still good. Then I had to help clean the potatoes. That took several days. We put some of them in the basement, and others we chopped in half to plant.

I was at that farm through the summer and fall. Each day there was a new challenge facing me that I needed to cope with: things that happened to others, things that happened to me. I probably have given too many such details already, although these experiences together describe something of the yoke I, with so many others, had to carry throughout that year in the Leoncin prison camp. Then in the late fall of 1946 the policemen at Leoncin said they didn't need all of us anymore, so some had to move on to different camps.

There was an officer in Leoncin who owned a farm some three kilometers from Sochaczew. He said he would take me with him to the camp there. So I walked 35 kilometers with him and his wife through the forest to Sochaczew. It was just the three of us on that trip. The policeman carried his long rifle over his shoulder. They had some food in a bag, and they each took a little more to eat than they gave me. But I must add, she was actually very nice, I enjoyed talking to her. She said, "We were ordered to treat you in this manner."

This couple also had a bike. One of them would ride the bike a kilometer or so ahead, and the other one would walk with me. They took turns, since there was only one bike and someone had to guard me. Even when I had to go behind the bushes or trees to the "bathroom," the woman would come with me to watch so I would not run away!

Many of the prisoners like me ran away when they had a chance. Many of them escaped while they were working on farms. They thought that if they were left in the basement for the winter, they would starve to death, so they had nothing to lose. I suppose I had the opportunity to run away too, but I couldn't. I was too scared. And I didn't know where I would go. I still held onto a glimmer of hope of seeing my family again. So I just thought I would wait and see what would happen. I knew life couldn't get any worse than it had already been.

When we approached the couple's farm, the wife said, "We will stop at our farm. We have a long row of potatoes hidden away." The potatoes were already dug, but as was the custom, they had put them in piles and covered them with straw and dirt to keep for the winter, and she wanted me to clean up those potatoes. I was to sort through them and throw away the rotten ones. They wanted to sell the others to make a little money. I soon discovered that most of the potatoes were rotten, so I had to sort them carefully. They were very cold, and my hands were freezing as I sorted them.

While I worked alone with those potatoes, the officer and his wife met up with some neighbors and had a little party, drinking whiskey and having fun. Close to evening, the woman told me to carry the cleaned and sorted potatoes into the shed. An older woman lived on the farm too, and she made us some soup for supper. When we finished eating, the wife said it was time to go to the big prison camp in Sochaczew.

So we continued walking. When we arrived in Sochaczew, the guards took me directly to another camp for prisoners. There were probably 100 people in this camp, it was much bigger than the one in Leoncin. There were some girls, some children, some young mothers, and soldiers who had been captured from East Prussia. It was a big group! The camp was set up as a collective farm like the ones in Russia. We worked there, growing food which was then taken to Russia on trains. But since it was late fall when I first arrived, we mostly worked inside.

The top commander at that camp was a Russian officer. He always wore a soldier's uniform. Below him was a Polish official who was called "Kerownik." He was a type of commander too. I believe it was the Communist government which was working in that building – probably the UBP. We could not ask, and we did not ask many questions, but I believe that is who it was. There were also many soldiers who marched around and tracked mud on their boots into the building. Sometimes the soldiers would beat some of the people. I did not get any beatings there, but they were very rough, just pushing us around and cursing. They called us "German swine," and called out to the older women, "you old whore, come here." We younger women were the "young whores." We got used to this, the normal talk each day.

One day the Russian officer came upon some soldiers beating up some prisoners, and he ordered them to stop. He said, "Put them to work, continue giving them their ration of food, but do not beat them anymore." After that the beating stopped. So we thought, that was a good Russian gentleman.

We worked in a big government building of four stories. Inside it looked like an office building. There were offices all around and a big corridor. Someone told us that it had been an office for the Germans when they were in power. Later on we found out that they kept Polish prisoners in part of the building while we were there. I guess they were the Poles who did not cooperate with the Communists.

The building was heated by big white *Kachelöfen* (tile ovens). In Poland at that time they did not have modern furnaces. In every room there was a Kachelofen. It stood in a corner, big and high, almost to the roof, and we would heat it pretty hot, so hot that even to warm my back against it was too warm. When the wood was burned, and only the coals were left, there was kind of a red glow. We had to close the door, and the heat would stay in that oven, and that was the heat for the whole day. That was enough until the next morning, since the heated *Kachel* (tiles) would then remain warm long into the night.

Throughout the fall and winter at Sochaczew, we prisoners were forced to load these ovens by hand since we had no baskets or boxes. We went to the forest and cut and gathered the wood, and loaded it onto trains which took it back to Russia.

Day after day we loaded the ovens with wood. We chopped the wood into smaller pieces so it would fit into the ovens, and when the fire was good and hot we added a bucket of coal. When the coal was glowing red, then we knew that the fire was ready and we could shut the oven doors. Each oven had double doors which we screwed tightly shut. That way the fire would last a long time.

Sometimes the wood was so wet, it was very hard to get it to burn. Sometimes it was even dripping! But still we had to light a fire with it. I would split wood into very fine pieces and put it behind the oven and it would dry a little bit and then the next day it would fire up much sooner.

At night the soldiers kept us in the basement of that building. We had only a little straw for our beds. They came at five o'clock in the morning to get us up and make us start to work. First we heated the ovens, and then we cleaned the floors every day, scrubbing them on our hands and knees. Oh, was that ever a job! The men smoked all day, and they flicked their ashes onto the floor. And they never used hankies to blow their noses; they just blew them onto the floor. It was so awful! But after a while I even got used to this and it seemed normal.

The office guards came in at 8:00, and by that time we had to have the ovens heated and the floors cleaned. By the time we were finished, we were all wet from sweating. Then they put us back in the basement for a few hours to rest. After that, we were sent out to the forest to chop wood. Day after day, that's what we did.

There was a Polish woman there who was in charge of us. She gave us orders as to how much wood to take to each oven, and when to wash the floors. She was a poor lady, but she was so good to us! She would sometimes sneak food to us, food that the guards had thrown away. She said to us, "Just do your work and someday things will get better for you." Her words gave us courage.

The whole building was full of government workers. The offices upstairs were mostly filled with guards who needed to report on the day's activities, prisoners' work assignments, and the names and number of incoming prisoners and of those sent to other camps. Some of these Poles were of the lower class. They were rough, very rough. I felt that they had their "claws" on us. But down below in the kitchen were women who cooked the meals. They were mostly poor Polish women, but most of them were nice to us. They did not yell at us or beat us. They let us do what we had to do, and left us alone.

One day, after I had fired the ovens, one of the office guards came to me and asked if I knew how to type. The prison office had a typewriter which the workers did not know how to use. I had learned in school the basics of typing, but was by no means an expert. These men, however, did not even know how to put the paper in! They did not know how to spell or write. Two of the big guards, with rifles on their backs, assumed some of us prisoners probably had some education, so they asked right away, "Who can type?" I thought, this sounds funny – you never know what the next question will be from them.

And one guard asked me, "Yrcka, Yrcka, can you type?"

I said, "Yes, but not too good."

"Could you come and help? I want to write a report, but do not know how to spell. And we are also having a little difficulty with the typewriter. It doesn't go."

He tried to put the paper in, but wasn't able. After I inserted the paper correctly, he tried to type, but did not know how to do it, not even how to space.

He then said, "You do it. There is not much to write, just the date, and what you did today. And at the bottom, you write your name."

So I as a prisoner actually sat down on a chair and began to type. My fingers were not so flexible, due to my winter work out in the forests, but I got it in and I said, "Here it is."

"Oh, thank you," he said, "you did a very good job."

Such was the Polish government at that time. The guard then put me down into the basement and shut the door. And there I was, again, in darkness.

We prisoners had no rights. We just had to follow orders. We could not say "Yes I will," or "No I won't," or "I don't want to."

It was hard to know how many prisoners were there at the same time. They split us up into groups. One group would go out to the forest to cut wood, and another group would stay inside to load the ovens. One group would be downstairs, working with the women in the kitchen, and one group would be working in the yard. The yard had a big barbed wire fence around it. And the guards walked around the edge of the fence, making sure we would not run away.

One time when we came in from cutting wood, we went into the kitchen where the cooks were tending large kettles full of soup. We watched them wheel those pots into the part of the building where they kept the prisoners. We didn't want to peek too much, but we looked down the hallway and saw the men behind the bars, waiting to be fed. The Polish girls who served them dished out the soup into deep bowls, like soldiers use. Then they slid the bowls under the bars to the men.

We worked in that office building, loading the ovens all winter. I was so thankful that the winter had not been colder than it was! I think if it had been really cold, we would not have survived. That basement was so cold, and we worked outside so much without enough food. Our hands and feet surely would have frozen, had it been a typical winter.

People were still buying prisoners for a bottle of whiskey or anything else they had to trade. The policemen would say, "You can have her for a week or two, but bring her back again." And sometimes the prisoners would not come back. We didn't know if they ran away, or if the Poles kept them, or if they were shot. We never saw them again.

The government building where we were imprisoned was on a large government farm. In the spring we planted onions, potatoes and sugar beets by hand. Then in the fall, we harvested these crops. Some of the sugar beets went to a nearby factory to make sugar. Most of them, however, we loaded onto trains and off they went to Russia.

It was more organized in this camp than before, but they still beat us when we were too slow. They gave us a good swat on our backs with a whip.

I remember we were so hungry that sometimes we would eat the onions that we were supposed to be planting. Every other onion went into our mouths. We smelled like onions – there was little to eat, and we were so hungry! In the morning we usually had coffee made from roasted barley, and a piece of bread. The bread wasn't very good, but we didn't mind, it tasted okay. For dinner we had a cabbage and potato soup – no meat, only vegetables. And for supper we were fed the same thing. Our meals were more regular than before, but we were still very hungry.

Our common eating utensils those years were simple tin cans. After the war ditches were filled with all sorts of tin cans. We took the lids off somehow, and this rusty can became our personal eating dish, in which our soup was served. For a few weeks we even had meat, when the 30 pigs on the farm contracted a disease, and had to be killed and buried. We uncovered these dead pigs, and found a stove and container that would boil the whole pig, and ate those dead pigs. Nobody died of disease that I know of. We prisoners gained a little bit of strength back, thanks to this meat, at least for a time.

At this farm we had to be deloused. They ran all of us through a kind of cold water shower, after which they put us through another place where we were sprayed with powder. We were so terrified of this, thinking this was poison – we had heard what the Jews' fate had been under the Germans. We thought this would be our end too. Powder was shooting at all of us. But it was simply delousing powder. We had to cover our eyes so the powder would not get in them. The powder was very potent, I guess. Then we went into a little pond nearby to wash it off.

The lice and bed bugs were so bad in all those camps, since we were sleeping in basements on straw. Oh, how those lice and mites itched and itched, until we almost went out of our minds – in the cracks between the fingers, behind the ears, elbows, head, everywhere! It was horrible. We picked the bed bugs out of the straw, but even so, they still crawled into our hair and onto our bodies. In the first camp they had cut off our hair, so that if we ran away people would know we were prisoners. Later we were allowed to let our hair grow, but this was also bad: long hair is awful when you have lice. I have never experienced this horrible form of torture, before my years in prison camp or since!

The Poles brought to this camp some German soldiers who were captured from the war. In the summer they were supposed to help make hay. But many of them were city boys and didn't know how to use the machines. When the boys were too slow, the officer kicked them and told them to work faster.

In the fall, we were taken to the fields to dig potatoes. We worked in a line, digging potatoes together. One of the German soldiers in particular was having a hard time keeping up. His name was Karl, and he was from Berlin. When the Polish officer wasn't looking, we would dig a plant or two from his row so he could keep up with us. We helped each other that way.

But I guess the Poles had their eyes on Karl anyway. One night they beat him up so badly – he was black and blue all over the next day. I don't know why they did it. It was probably just plain madness. We were all frightened by their madness. We didn't know what would happen to us next. Everybody was afraid that we would be sent to Siberia. This was the common talk among the Poles, threatening to send us to Siberia and letting us die there.

Soon thereafter, Karl and four others planned to run away. Karl told me, "I've already been imprisoned twice, and will escape again." But it was so dangerous. The Poles would shoot those who ran away. There was a German prisoner from Königsberg in East Prussia, and a girl too. I can see that girl like it was yesterday. Her name was Maria. She was kind of tough, like a soldier. She wore a pair of soldier's shoes that she had found someplace. She wore them day and night so that nobody could steal them from her, or at least they would have to fight her if they tried.

Maria said to me, "I'm not staying here!" Yet all the time she would also say, "But where should I go, without clothes, without money, without bread?" All of us were wearing old civilian clothes, but they were in tatters. She did not have soldier clothes, but in my opinion I took her to be a German soldier. She was kind of like a man in her character, and she said, "Edna, you are stupid if you remain here; I'm going along!"

For days they didn't eat the bread they were given. Instead, they stuck it under their shirts, and saved it for when they would run away. They whispered to me, asking me to come with them. They didn't know Polish as well as I did, so they wanted me to come along to translate. But I was afraid. Maria ran away with those German soldiers one night, but I stayed behind. Then I was alone at the farm.

This is not the end of the episode. A month or so later, a letter arrived from Berlin. It was from Karl and he wrote: "The Polish Government need not search for us any longer." He had actually addressed that letter to this camp, and the letter arrived! A guard whose name was Karl Block came to me. The name sounds German, but he was Polish and had been a good friend of my Dad. He too was a *Dorfschulze*. They attended meetings together, and he knew I was David Schroeder's daughter.

Karl Block said, "Look, Edna, what these Germans did. Now we will not be hunting for them anymore." And I wondered, what is he trying to tell me? Should I be happy about it? I just looked at him, without expression. And I thought to myself, whether or not I should appear happy – I was indeed happy for them that they made it, but I could not show it, otherwise he might say, Oh I see you are happy for them that they went. And at the same time I was a little sorry that I had decided not to go along with them.

How these five Germans made it, I do not know. They were wearing nothing but rags, but they made it. But the men said, after the war in the Ukraine they had been imprisoned by the Russians twice before and had managed to escape. And here for a third time they also escaped, and had the nerve to write a letter to this camp that the Poles need not look for them any longer, they were safe at home. And when that Karl Block showed me that letter, I said to myself, what to do now? I was just tough like a rock: I did not blink an eye, I just looked straight ahead and then simply went my way, filled with terror.

By this time it was late fall, 1947, and it started to snow a little bit. My only possessions were my clothes, the rags on my feet, and a little knife. After the others escaped, the policeman brought me to piles of sugar beets. I had to cut the green leaves off of the beets, and throw them on a pile. I think they didn't know what to do with me then, since I was alone.

I worked on those beets all morning, my hands were freezing, but I thought, Well, it has to be done. That afternoon a big heavy military truck came by, driven by a German chauffeur and with four policemen on the back. I wondered what would happen then, perhaps they would shoot me. We were kind of prepared for anything and everything. I looked up at them from my piles of beets. One of the men told me to hop on the back of the truck. And there I stood: dirty hands, half-frozen. I recognized the chauffeur; he was a boy who had grown up in our village. He was still a prisoner too, and was working as a chauffeur and mechanic. The Polish people didn't know how to take care of their trucks, so they used German prisoners. I don't remember what I did with the little knife I had in my hand. Maybe I just left it there on the ground.

I hopped onto the back of the truck and we drove towards Warsaw.

FINDING 🏠 SHELTER

We had to pass through several checkpoints before reaching Warsaw. I found out that the policemen I was with in the truck were members of the PPR party, which had just taken control of the government. PPR soldiers set up posts on the roads and checked the people who were coming and going. They held us up at one checkpoint for a long time, but finally they let us through.

It wasn't far to Warsaw – maybe 30 kilometers or so. When we got there, they took me to another camp for prisoners. This camp was even a little better than the others, it was the largest prison camp yet. Here we were kept in military-style barracks.

The policemen first took me to an office at the camp to get me registered. There was a civilian behind a desk, a blonde man who looked familiar to me. With a second glance, I recognized him as someone I had known from before the war, eight years earlier. He had aged, of course, and I couldn't remember his name, but I knew that he had known my Dad pretty well. His family, the Kwiatkowskis, were the ones we stayed with when we brought the fruit to Warsaw to sell. Mr. Kwiatkowski would say to us "Just stay here with us for the night." So Dad and I would sleep on mattresses in their house.

He didn't know who I was at first, either. We both had changed quite a bit since the last time Dad and I came to Warsaw together. Then he looked at my papers and saw my name, "Schroeder." He looked up at me and asked who my father was.

"David Schroeder," I said.

"Oh, you're Edna, that little blonde girl!" he said.

He wrote all my information down, and then sent me on to the camp.

All the prisoners at this camp wore the same clothing – a greenish gray uniform. That way people would recognize us as prisoners if we tried to leave the camp. It was like a very straight robe, with buttons down the front and a little collar at the top.

For the first few months they made us clean up the rubble where the Jewish ghetto had been. Early in the war, the Germans had cordoned off a large piece of Warsaw, transforming it into a Jewish ghetto. Later, when the Russians were approaching Warsaw, the Germans supposedly still had 6,000 Jews to transfer by train to Dachau or Auschwitz, but they could not make it. They had run out of time, the Russians were pushing so fast. So the Germans sent airplanes and bombed the ghetto. There were bomb craters everywhere, holes within holes. And we were supposed to clean up the rubble.

Some Catholic priests wanted to rebuild the Polish Catholic Cathedral that was destroyed in this blitz. It had been the biggest church in Warsaw. We helped with that too. (Later, in 1972, my sister returned to Warsaw. She told me that the same cathedral which I had helped to rebuild was still standing there.)

There were at least 300 other prisoners working with me – mostly women, almost no men. Older women also were forced to work, and even children, eight or ten years old, were hard at work. We worked from dawn to dusk, cleaning up the ghetto. We women were the *Trümmmerfrauen* (rubble women), the work force that operated the *Backsteinmühle* (rubble mill). We worked mostly with our hands, tearing down the charred walls of the gutted buildings, brick by brick. When we would find here and there a good brick – there were not very many – they had to be chopped out nicely and set aside, so they could be used again.

A few of the other Trümmmerfrauen had shovels, some had picks, and some had hammers, but most of us had no tools except for our hands. We had little handcarts into which we loaded the bricks and things. The bricks that were too broken were taken outside the city on the train tracks and dumped. We worked so hard at this camp! But at least the soldiers treated us better than before. And a few of the younger Polish priests helped out by pushing the little handmade wagons on train tracks.

That man from the registration office who knew my Dad had a little bit of power, and he said he could shuffle things around a bit for me. He arranged for me to work for his mother in her store close to Josef's church, on Marszałkowska Street, the main street of

Warsaw. I remembered exactly how this street had looked before the war.

Warsaw had been terribly damaged by the war. Most of the buildings had been hit by bombs or gunfire, and there was rubble everywhere. Even the store was mostly destroyed, it was just a shack. But at that time, such stores were normal. People just made do and arranged things so they would have a bit of shelter, even while bricks and boards were falling down around them.

In the morning an armed guard brought me from the camp to the store. People in the streets would just look on as we walked past. In the evening the guard would march me back to the camp. I wore my prison uniform to work, but in the store I put on a store uniform on top that partially covered the prison garb.

They set me to work packing butter, cleaning fish, and sweeping snow and ice off the sidewalks. At night I closed the windows with boards. Sometimes when they had a lot of extra work to do, they paid the guard a little bribe and he allowed me to spend the night at the store. Sometimes I even stayed a couple of nights, packing butter, and cleaning chickens, ducks and rabbits in the basement so they would be ready for the next day. The store owner told the guard to keep me registered at the camp, but to let me stay there all night to work. At first I didn't know how they arranged this, but then I found out about the bribe.

I also found out that the Kwiatkowskis were trading on the black market. My eyes were opened to a lot of things there! They received flour from the United States – nice white flour that was supposed to be given to the poor people, but they would sell it for a better price to the rich people who had money to pay for it. This happened a lot after the war. I would pack this flour in two, five and ten pound gray bags, place it under the counter in the store, and the wealthy customers would come and buy this flour. They didn't mind the higher price.

The Kwiatkowskis sold butter on the black market too. The farmers brought their butter in to sell by the piece. We sold both white and yellow butter, but the yellow was very popular. The farmers added a little carrot juice to the butter to make it nice and yellow. Then they brought it rolled up in rhubarb leaves and then wrapped in newspaper.

I would carry the butter into the Kwiatkowskis' house across the street – one of the few houses that had not been destroyed. Almost all the buildings otherwise had been completely gutted. The house was kept very warm, so the butter would get really soft. I put the butter in the bathtub, and kneaded it like bread to make it all one color. Then we would pack it with a wooden mold and paper. We put the paper in, and then the butter, and we formed it into nice cakes.

In the morning we took about 25 lbs. at a time and sold this grade one butter to the rich people who came to the store for double the usual price. We would only take that much because they were afraid the police would catch them and give them a fine. So when we ran out, I would go back to the house and bring more. We kept it under the counter, and when the upper class people came in, they would ask for grade one butter.

I also worked, reluctantly, with the fish. There was a big barrel full of live fish, which we sold. The other girls who worked there didn't want to touch the fish, so that was my job even though I hated the smell of fish. A foreign gentleman came into the store pretty regularly and asked for fish. I later found out he was the Danish Consul. I had to reach into the barrel and get out a fish, and then hit it on the head to kill it. I did not like to kill those poor fish, but I had to do it. This took some getting used to! Then I would wrap it in paper for that gentleman. He would often give me a little present for getting the fish for him. Sometimes he put a piece of chocolate into the pocket in my shirt, and sometimes he put some chewing gum. But I didn't know what chewing gum was, so I didn't know what to do with it.

Even though I was working in that store, I continued to need to wear the prison uniform that they gave us at that camp in Warsaw. This greenish-gray dress told everyone that I belonged to the prison camp. People looked at me funny, but I got used to it. By that time women in Warsaw were wearing fur coats and earrings. Some parts of the city had recovered a bit from the war. It was the end of 1947.

After a while the Kwiatkowski's son from the registration office would come home in the evenings and talk to me about taking Polish citizenship. He said, "Things are getting better for you, and you are in the category of people who can take Polish citizenship.

Then you wouldn't have to stay in the prison camp anymore. Anyone from 18 to 25 years of age is eligible, this includes you."

Oh, I thought, that sounds pretty good. Finally I could be released from prison!

After thinking about it overnight in the prison camp, I talked to him again and asked, "Can I really get my rights back? I would like to go back to school, since I was just in the seventh grade when the war brought an end to all schooling."

"Yes," he said, "when you get your Polish citizenship, you can even get work here in Warsaw in our store, earning regular wages like they pay the other two girls working here."

Around this same time, other people were also starting to talk about Polish citizenship. People in the prison camp said that if we would get citizenship, things would be better for us. I thought that might be a good idea. If I could get out of prison, maybe I could get a job and earn some money, find a little place to live, and continue my schooling. Then I could start looking for my family. I didn't know where my mother and sister were, but if I got out of the prison camp, maybe I could find them and we could start over. Some people even said we could return to our farms from before the war. But I thought I wouldn't want to go there where people still knew me. I just wanted to find my family and have a little freedom.

When we were in the prison camps, we didn't have any rights. I thought if I could get out of the camps, I could start rebuilding my life. Polish citizenship seemed like my ticket to a life that was a little more free,. I found out later that by that time the law that prisoners could apply for citizenship had been in effect for several years already. But they kept it kind of quiet because we were cheap labor, and if we became free, they would have to start paying us real wages. In any case, I was at a turning point in my life: I wanted to live! And I was certain there was not a future for me in this prison camp.

Taking citizenship sounded like a good idea, but I wasn't sure it was the right thing to do. In the back of my mind, I wondered if the borders would be open some day and I could go to Germany or somewhere else. But finally I decided I would try to get Polish citizenship. The main thing I wanted to do was find my family, and then go back to school.

I went to the government office where we were registered

when I first came to Warsaw. They gave me some papers to fill out before I could get my citizenship. On one of the papers I had to collect the signatures of 20 people who knew me during the war. They had to testify about my behavior when Germany was in power. The government wanted to know if I was in Hitler's party, if I had persecuted the Polish people or the Jews, if I had turned anyone in to the police, that sort of thing.

So I thought I would go back to my village and see if any of my Polish friends, teachers, and neighbors were still alive. I got leave from the camp to collect signatures. They gave me a little paper saying that I was allowed to travel. And then, all of a sudden, I thought about what my Mom had told me when I was in the Hitler camps. She told me not to wear my uniform home, not to let the neighbors see me wearing it. So they never knew that I was in those camps! I knew I could find people who would testify that I had not been a Nazi.

When I told the two girls, Sofia and Maria, who worked at the store about my intentions, they said, "You cannot go in those clothes you have on; everybody will know who you are."

So one of them lent me shoes to wear. The owner's daughter, Yadja, gave me a dress and other things. And I set off to collect the signatures.

I headed back to my village, Secymin. I walked from Warsaw, past our old church, and on. At the church, I saw lots of children running around the building. Then suddenly, I found myself crying. The church windows were broken, some windows had cardboard stuck in them, one window had a board leading up to it where chickens were entering. The nice fence was torn down. It was so sad! Then I walked past my grandparents' old house, and the Nickels' place, and the Bartels' place. I knew them all as a little girl.

It was a blustery cold day, and a storm came up, quite suddenly. This was already January 1948. Soon it really started to rain and snow. I was getting cold and wet, so I looked for some kind of shelter. On this road I passed a shack that I remembered from before. Back then there were poor Polish people living in it.

I knew I couldn't go in my grandparents' house, or to the Nickels' house. Polish people were living in them now. And at Bartels' place, Polish children were running around and playing. So I thought

I would just hide in that shack until the clouds passed over. The door to the shack was partly open. There was just a little straw in there, and clay on the bottom. I opened the inner door, and an old lady came out.

I could see past her into a small room. There was an old man lying on the straw in the corner, on a blanket. In the other corner they had put in a sort of kitchen stove – some old bricks and a piece of rusted tin on top and a little pipe through the top.

I thought I recognized the couple, but they were much older than I remembered. The woman seemed quite scared, and she was trying to speak to me in a little Polish. Many of the older Mennonites didn't know Polish very well. The younger generation had a bit more schooling, and we learned Polish that way. "What would you like?" she said, in broken Polish. I said, "It's raining and snowing, could I come in just until the clouds blow over?" And she said sure, it would be fine. But she kept standing in the doorway to the second room. She didn't let me go in any farther towards her husband.

Then suddenly I knew who they were. They were Heinrich Bartel and his wife. They had been my grandparents' neighbors! I had not seen them for almost ten years. I was certain that's who they were, but I waited to see how we would communicate. And then he said to his wife, "Wea es doa?" That was Low German, "Who is there?" And she responded in Low German, "Oh, it's just a young girl. It's raining and snowing outside, and she wants to come in." So I could understand them, but I had forgotten my Low German, so I couldn't respond. But I asked them in High German, "Are you Heinrich Bartels?" "Yes," they said, "Und wer bist Du?" I told them I was Erna Schroeder, "Peter Schroeder was my grandfather, your neighbor." Then she got all excited. "Du bist die kleine Erna Schroeder? – You are little Erna with the curly blonde hair?" Although my name was Edna, Erna was my nickname. I had often spent my school holidays at my grandparents' house, and had known the Bartels quite well. But by now I had grown up – I was 21!

So she let me in and we started catching up about all that had happened since the war. I told her I was collecting signatures to get my Polish citizenship. And she said, "Ah, child, don't do it!" I told her I wanted to go to school. But she just looked at me like it was a big sin, what I was doing. I started to feel scared.

But then she said, "Come sit here on the straw, and I will make you a cup of tea." I thought, Where did she get tea? She went behind her husband, to a little hole and brought out powdered milk, powdered egg, and a tin of tea. Since it was snowing outside, she went out and collected some snow in an empty tin can, and began melting it on the fire she built in the stove. When the water was hot, she sprinkled in the tea and some sugar, and stirred it with a little stick. And then she brought out some nice crackers. We also ate lunch together. I don't remember what she made. She took a little water and milk powder, I guess, and egg powder – she had a little rusty frying pan. During the meal, she asked how I was, how I had stayed alive, and where my parents were. We had a good visit.

All the time she was doing this, she kept saying how I shouldn't take the citizenship. Oh, she went with her eyes, rolling them back, saying, "Aber Kind (but child), don't do that, don't do that." Then I was a little confused. I thought Polish citizenship would grant me freedom; I could go to school, and live a free life like before the war.

I had also asked her where she got all the tea. And she told me the secret. "There are Americans who gave it. They come each month delivering food so we can stay alive; otherwise there is no food around." She put her finger to her mouth, and said I should tell no one. A light went on for me then. I thought, "I have an uncle in America." Maybe I could make contact with these Americans.

"Are they in Warsaw?" I asked.

"No," she said. "Farther up, near Danzig. They come once a month and give us blankets and clothes, and some food," she said.

The Bartels kept this food hidden in a hole under the blanket and the straw where Mr. Bartel slept, so that their Polish neighbors wouldn't find out and wonder where it came from, and perhaps steal it. So she told me about MCC – the Mennonite Central Committee – those American Mennonites who were going to the camps to find Mennonite refugees. She told me it would be better if I would put my name on the list that one of the Americans had. Maybe I could then get out of Poland, into Germany, and then on to Canada or to the States.

The Bartels gave me the MCC address in Pelplin, and told me to get in touch with them somehow. So as I left the shack, I struggled over what to do: continue gathering those 20 signatures, or stop and wait to hear from MCC. I thought I would get the rest of my signatures anyway, then I would have them. The gentleman at the prison camp was expecting the signatures, and he would wonder why I stopped getting them. But I knew I would try to contact MCC, and maybe find another way.

I left the Bartels, and walked the rest of the way to my village. I found some old neighbors, school friends, workers, and one Polish farmer who was in our village, and asked them to sign for me. I even found Sofia, the neighbor girl who had worked for us. Many people were surprised to find that I was still alive. One family even asked me to spend the night with them. But I was afraid. I thought maybe others would find out and report me to the police.

Then I decided to try to find my teacher, the one who had told me our ways would part. I only needed a few more signatures. She lived near Sochaczew about 35 kilometers away, near a forest. So I set off to find her.

She was very surprised to see me! When I told her I was trying to get Polish citizenship, she looked at me gravely and said in a quiet voice, "Edna, you have good plans, but I think you should not do it." She said, "If you get Polish citizenship, the border will be closed to you for certain, especially since you are German. I think it would be better if you tried to find a way out of Poland. I know your parents have some relatives in Canada or the United States; they can help you find your way out of Poland." She gave me her signature, but her words stayed with me.

I had my 20 signatures by then, so I set off from my teacher's house to return to Warsaw. She packed me a sandwich for the trip. When I arrived at the camp, I turned my papers in to the authorities. So I was very close to getting my Polish citizenship. But I started to have second thoughts about it.

I couldn't sleep very well those days. A voice was telling me to write to the Americans first. The Bartels had given me an address that I memorized. Had I not gone for those signatures, and into that shack, I never would have known about MCC. They gave me the address: MCC, Rolin, Pelplin. In Poland we have a thread that was called MCC sewing thread, so I remembered that right away. But Rolin, Pelplin, I could not put down on paper. I didn't want to write

it down, in case someone would find it on me, and even if I had
wanted to, I did not have a pen. So while I was walking, I repeated
endlessly to myself, "Rolin, Pelplin". I kind of sang it over and over
to myself as I walked: "MCC, Rolin, Pelplin," "MCC, Rolin, Pelplin."
And that's all I needed.

The Bartels had explained to me that MCC was sort of like
the Red Cross. They helped people by giving out clothes and food.
And I was looking for help! I had no shoes, and no clothes: just my
prison uniform. I didn't have stamps, or any paper, or pencil, or an
envelope – nothing. So upon my return, I went to the girls in the
store and asked them to help me.

Those girls were so nice to me! They helped me out just like
I was part of their family. I told them I wanted to write to the Red
Cross to see if I can find my Dad and my Mom and my family. Perhaps the Red Cross could contact my uncle in America, who might
have some family information. I took a piece of paper and a pencil
into the back room where the bags of flour were, and there I wrote
that letter. One girl responded, saying, "See, we are good friends, we
are like three good friends." We spoke to each other in Polish, always.

I don't remember much of what I wrote. I probably asked
them if they could help me, and I gave my name and address. I did
mention that the owner of the store called me "Yrcka," since my real
name, Edna, sounded too German. So I wrote that they should ask
for Yrcka.

One of the girls, Sofia, said that she had some errands to run
for the store, and she would be glad to take the letter, put a stamp on
it and send it. I didn't know if it would reach the right people, or if
there even was such a place. Then I said a little prayer. I prayed,
"Lord, please take this letter and send it where it needs to go."

CH • 6

THE LIGHT IS COMING

It didn't take long before I received an answer to my prayer. Maybe only two or three days later, Bob Fisher, a volunteer with MCC, came into the store. He walked straight to the counter where I was working – I was weighing sugar or flour or something – and held up my letter so I could see my own handwriting. He said he was looking for Yrcka. The owner probably thought he was another foreign gentleman, like the Danish Consul, wanting to buy a fish or something. They had tea and coffee in the store, but they would not sell it to Polish people, only to foreigners who would pay them more money.

In the back of my mind I thought, "Now I am in trouble!" I had lived for so many years without trusting anyone, and now I trusted someone I had never met before. I was terribly afraid and excited at the same time. This seemed to be an answer to my prayer, but yet when I saw this American, I was afraid that he was a spy sent to check me out – to see if I really wanted to take the citizenship.

The letter had arrived at the MCC house just before Bob was to leave for Warsaw on other business, so it worked perfectly for him to come find me. I was working behind the counter, and I looked up to see who was coming in the door. I usually didn't pay any attention to who was coming in and going out, but for some reason, I looked up. He came straight to me, my letter in hand. He asked quietly in half Polish, half German, "Yrcka Schroeder?" I said, "yes," in Polish. Then he asked me in broken German if I spoke German. "Oh," I thought, as soon as I saw him, "this is my chance to escape."

It was as if a light had come on just for me. But I was so afraid of men! I thought, this matter is too close, too personal, it needs to be woman to woman. But for some reason I was no longer scared. Bob said to me, "I, Rolin, Pelplin," or something like that. So I knew he was from MCC. And when he said, "I have a wife, Rachel," I told myself, I need to meet that wife! This motivated me. Scared or not, I will go with this man, meet his wife, and maybe they can help me.

So I went to Mrs. Kwiatkowski and told her that there was a man from the Red Cross who was looking for my family. I lied again. I didn't say that I had written him and asked him for help. The girls knew, but she did not.

Bob was very smart. He saw some apples there in the store, and so he picked up a few, put them in a bag, and brought them to the counter to pay for them. That way he endeared himself to the woman. I asked her if I could go and talk to him, and she agreed – "but only for a half hour," she said. So Bob and I went outside.

We walked out of the store and down the street, past two or three bombed-out buildings to the Kwiatkowski's house. Bob started to talk, and he told me he had a suitcase with clothes in it for me. He said, "Just go try them on." I tried everything on, and most of it fit – even shoes and underwear! At that point I thought I was so rich, since I had some clothes to wear. There was also a blanket and a sweater and a black shawl made of wool. Later, I sewed a beautiful dress out of that shawl. There was so much nice stuff in that suitcase – even hankies! I later found out these clothes were from the bales of clothing and blankets gathered by North American Mennonites as part of the MCC post-war relief work.

Bob and I sat and talked. We both tried to use High German, but his was broken, and mine was broken. Even so, somehow we connected. Then the half hour was up and one of the owner's children came by to get me.

Bob gave me 300 zlotys. "Just hide it, so no one can see," he said, "maybe it will help you to buy some things you need." I hadn't had any money in years. Nothing. The clothing he brought was so nice, but here was money too!

Then Bob said he would try to come back in the evening to talk some more. So I told Mrs. Kwiatkowski that he would be coming back in the evening. She asked me about who he was and what he was doing. I simply told her he was with a group like the Red Cross, and they were trying to connect families. I said I had an uncle in America, and maybe we could establish some contact through letters. She didn't say anything.

Finally she agreed that I could spend an hour talking with him, but then I would have to go back to the prison camp. So Bob came by a little before the end of my workday. I was upstairs at their home, working with the butter, but she let me leave early. Downstairs, the children were already eating supper. Bob later said he was so interested to see what they were eating. They had some rolls and some sausage, and tea. I thought this was a pretty good meal, but Bob thought it was an unusual combination.

As we were talking, I asked him where he came from, and told him about my uncle in America. He told me about his wife in Rolin, Pelplin. I thought I would love to see his wife and to have her as a friend. But how could I? I was a poor refugee, and she was *Amerikanisch*. So I asked Bob, "Herr Fisher, can I go with you to your MCC?" And he said, yes, I could.

I don't know where it came from, but I just knew that's what I would do. I guess the Lord gave me those words to say, and the strength to go through with it. Immediately we started to plan. How would we get on the train, how would we keep the police from finding out who I was? On the trains, the police checked everybody's passport. But we just thought we could do it somehow.

The train station was a few kilometers outside of Warsaw, and I didn't know how we would even get there. But Bob said he would call a friend of his in Warsaw. I was surprised when I found out that his friend was the Danish Consul – the man who came into the store regularly and had me kill fish for him! So we agreed on a time to meet with him, and agreed that Bob would come to the house and ask permission to take me away for a few days. So that's what we did.

Mrs. Kwiatkowski thought that since I was trying to get my papers in order to become a Polish citizen, that perhaps this had something to do with that. So she let me go. She wondered where I was going, and I said, close to Danzig; I would be going by train. Then she said, "Promise you will come back in three days." And I promised. Another lie! Since I often stayed at the Kwiatkowskis for one or more nights when there was extra work, this is probably how Mrs. Kwiatkowski was able to grant me this unusual permission.

Bob and I left that evening – at 7:00 or so. Bob had phoned the Danish Consul, who came to meet us with a car and drove us to the train station. I still cannot believe how we got on that train and made it all the way to Danzig without any papers. Bob was very confident. He said we would just try it, and if there was any problem, he would say that he wanted to hire me for a few days to do housework or something. Later I thought, they could have put me in jail – but I was already a prisoner. But Bob had a wife and relatives, and if he had sat in jail because of me, I would have felt terrible! They could even have arrested him for being a spy, and gotten MCC into a lot of trouble!

At the train station, Bob said, "Just put your arm in mine, and we'll pretend you are my wife." I thought, I never would have done that in normal times – taken the arm of a man. But I did it. I tell my children sometimes, you can do things in war time that you would not do in normal times. In normal times I don't see people dying all around me. In wartime I would walk over dead people and think nothing of it. We got used to that. We just walked over them and thought that they were lucky to be dead rather than alive. We did what we had to do.

I took Bob's arm and we walked to the station. We came to the gate and a policeman stopped us. Bob took out his passport, and said I was his wife. I must have looked nice since I was wearing the clothes Rachel sent. So he let us get on the train without asking for my papers. When we got on the train, the conductor came around to get our tickets and look at our passports. Bob paid for the tickets and took his passport out again. The conductor said, "Okay, good enough," and he never even asked for mine! Since Bob's passport was in English, he couldn't read it, so he just looked at it and went on.

Bob told me to pretend I was sleeping. He bought a Polish newspaper and pretended to read it, page after page. The conductor came around again, but passed us by. Then a Polish man came on the train; he had spent some time in England, so he knew a few words in English, and talked a bit with Bob.

When we got off the train, there was another policeman who checked Bob's passport, and let us through. There was someone waiting for us with a jeep – someone from MCC, but I forget who it was. We drove a while in that jeep until we reached the MCC house in Pelplin. We had made it!

It did not take me long to find out that at MCC, I had indeed entered a different world from the one I had known for almost a decade. I soon came to the conclusion that I would rather be shot than to go back to the darkness of prison camps anymore.

Rachel Fisher came out to meet me in her wine-colored morning coat. I thought she was really rich, with her long black hair. She looked like an angel! She greeted me in German and took me inside the house.

It was breakfast time, so I washed up a bit and looked around. There were ten MCC workers living in the house at that time. Many of them had come to Poland to work with MCC's tractor project. MCC had sent tractors to help with the recovery after the war, and they also sent people to help teach the farmers how to use the tractors and how to take care of them.

The MCC unit was so different from anything I had experienced since the outbreak of the war. The whole atmosphere was different. Right away everyone was nice to me. People were so gentle, so friendly, and tried to help in any way they could. There were Bibles, and we had devotions before we ate. That was like medicine for my heart! I could not understand the words, since it was in English, but it felt so nice anyway. I never again wanted to face the darkness of my previous years.

Then Menno Fast said, "Which songs should we sing? *Gott ist die Liebe?*" I knew that song from when I was a little girl. Rachel played the piano while we sang, and I felt like I was already in America!

Rachel prepared breakfast for us. She came to me and asked so gently, "Ein Ei oder zwei?" She said it in broken German, but I knew what she meant. I thought, "Eggs for breakfast?" I hadn't seen that for years! I asked for only one egg, because I thought I shouldn't take more than that. They fed me bread and milk, and that was so good, but then lots more food came.

After breakfast we talked about what I should do. In three days I had to go back to Warsaw again. Menno said that if I had a birth certificate, he could put me on a list and most likely help me get out of Poland to Germany or somewhere. But without papers, there was not much we could do.

Menno was helping a lot of people get out of Poland at that time. He went into the camps and found Mennonites, and made all the arrangements to help them get out. And those people I found in the shack, the Bartels, they got out that way. They had their birth certificates and other papers.

But I had no papers. I had left them at my house when the Polish soldiers took me to the first camp. In the excitement, I never even thought about carrying papers with me. But even if I had, the soldiers certainly would never have permitted me to take such papers along. In any case, I had nothing, so MCC couldn't put me on their list.

I arrived at the MCC house on the 11th of February, 1948, and I never went back to Warsaw. The Polish government didn't find me. I don't think they knew where to look. I had told the people in the store that I was going with the Red Cross to Danzig. They trusted Bob and that Danish Consul, and so they let me go. I think that since I had started to get my Polish citizenship, they trusted me even more. They probably thought I was trying to get all the details worked out. But I never went back. I keep wondering what sort of punishment Mrs. Kwiatkowski had to suffer on my account. This weighs heavily upon me to this day.

Bob and Rachel and all the other MCC workers were so nice to me! I began to see a different way to live. I carried hope that somehow I would be able to escape Poland. Rachel was especially kind. We had trouble with communication since we didn't speak the same language, but I could tell that our hearts and minds were in the same place. I began to trust. We were so close – she was like a sister to me and she loved me. It felt so good when she hugged me. I wasn't used to hugs, because it had been such a long time since I had been with anyone who loved me. And it wasn't the fashion or custom during the war years to hug people.

Soon after I arrived in Pelplin, Rachel asked me if I would like to take a bath and wash my hair. During all those years in the camps I didn't have a chance to wash my hair or to really get clean. So I gave myself a thorough washing with Rachel's good soap. My hair was naturally very wavy, but since it hadn't been washed for so long, it stayed quite flat. After I washed it, it puffed up and was so fluffy and wavy. Then I wondered what I could do to tame it! In a couple days it calmed down again, and it felt so much better, so light and clean.

The house at Pelplin was fairly big. The land around it was a state farm. The farm offices were in half of the building, and MCC used the other half. There were big rooms on the bottom, and on the top were smaller bedrooms. Before the war it had belonged to a wealthy family. When the Russians came in they wanted to make everything level between the rich and the poor, so they took it over and made it into a state-run farm, growing mostly grain – wheat and rye – and some potatoes. The bread we ate was always the brown kind, made from rye. There were large fields of potatoes, and barley, and oats.

On one side of the house was a large room where the MCC workers stored the big piles of food which came off the boat from America. I remember seeing cans full of beef, peaches, milk powder, and egg powder. There were piles of blankets, too. All of these things were for the people in Poland, to help them recover from the war.

I thought it was good of the government to let MCC use the building. They were always very nice to Americans, though. The overseer of the farm was an officer, but he always went around in civilian clothes. I think he was probably a member of the Communist party. He wasn't like a police officer or a soldier, he was a civilian. But he gave the orders about what should be planted, and he kept the books. So he was above the workers.

I know he probably kept an eye on MCC, but I remember that he was a nice man. He and his wife lived in the other half of the building, but they mostly kept to themselves. They kept some cows, and sometimes they gave us milk for our cooking. Ruth Miller did most of the cooking for the house, and she told me to take a container to the Polish officer each evening and ask for a little milk. I could walk through the house to get there. There was a hallway, and a door, and behind that door was their living quarters.

So I went and I said, "Good evening. May I have some milk?"

That's all I said. And they didn't ask me any questions. They just smiled at me. Sometimes I would forget to go until morning, and then I had to run quickly to them and ask them for milk before breakfast. If they had some extra, they would give us a little. Otherwise we would have our porridge without milk.

Aside from this interaction, I took care to stay hidden from the neighbors. I was so thankful to be there, but I was also very scared. I thought that since I left Warsaw illegally, the police would try to catch me and take me to jail. Sometimes when people would run away, the police would bring them back and torture or kill them right away. So that was always in the back of my mind – I lived half in peace and half in fear.

I left the house only a few times during my stay. For many years I hadn't had a toothbrush or toothpaste, and my teeth needed attention. So Rachel took me to a dentist to have my teeth fixed. We went to a woman dentist in Elbing (today, Elblag). She was German, but the Poles had given her the right to open an office there. For a while I went to see her once or twice a week – sometimes I went with the Fishers, sometimes with Menno Fast. The workers had a little jeep which they used to get around, it was like an army jeep.

The dentist had a foot pedal that she used to power her drill. She drilled and drilled on my teeth. It was really painful, because she didn't use any Novocain. But pain or no pain, it had to be done. She filled cavities and cleaned my teeth. They were in very bad shape, but she fixed them nicely.

While I was in Pelplin, I helped out by doing some chores around the house. There was a girl named Yadja who worked in the house too. She was from the village and she was Polish. I was very careful around her. She was very easy to get along with, and she never asked me many questions. She may have not even known I was a German.

One day I made a funny mistake. The MCC workers had their clothes sent to town for laundering. They came back washed and nicely folded in boxes. Each worker's name was written on tags on the back of the clothes to help with sorting them out. Sometimes I helped write the names on the clothes and sometimes I helped to sort them.

We sorted the clothes on a big table downstairs, and arranged them in piles. Then we took the piles upstairs and laid them on the beds for each person. One day Yadja was sorting the freshly-washed clothes, but then she was called away to do something else. So I started sorting by myself.

I didn't know much English, but I wanted to learn. I had picked up a few words, but I couldn't really read, since the sounds and the spelling were so different from Polish. I could see the names on the tags and make out whose they were. Fisher was a German name, so I could recognize that name. When I sorted the hankies – the red ones, like farmers use – it seemed strange to me that all the hankies belonged to Mr. Fast. I addressed people by their last names, "Mr. Fast" or "Mr. Fisher," and I thought maybe Mr. Fast's first name was actually Karl or something like that (only finding out later it was "Menno").

So I took the piles of clothes up to the rooms and placed all the hankies on Menno's bed. A little later in the day he came down and said, "We got our clothes today, and it seems that I got all the hankies."

I said, "Yes, I did that. They have your name on them." I was even proud that I could read a little bit.

Then he looked at me kind of funny and all of a sudden he started laughing. The labels said "Color fast!" We laughed for a while and then he went upstairs and sorted them out himself.

I had never seen people who smiled so much! Everyone in the house was so friendly and they laughed at things that because of my poor English I didn't understand. I thought, these people must not have many worries, that they can laugh so much. All through the war I didn't laugh at all. I thought I would never laugh again.

I also saw how earnestly they prayed when they had devotions. And I needed that. I was so hungry, so empty. We had devotions every day before breakfast. They each took a turn leading the devotions, even the women. Sometimes we sang songs with the piano, and that was new to me too. I had never seen a piano before in Poland. I had seen little organs with pedals, but no pianos. Young people in Poland often played music – guitars and fiddles. But our family wasn't very musical, so we never had those in the house.

Menno was the one who usually went out to the camps to look for Mennonites. He worked to reunite families and to help people find a way to leave the camps and go to the West. The government didn't know too much about what he was doing, and he had to be careful. Eventually they started to become suspicious of the unit. Other MCC workers also took food and blankets to orphanages as well as to the camps.

I didn't usually accompany Menno on his trips to the camps, of course. But once I went with him to visit my Aunt Wanda. Menno had her name on a list, she was in a big camp in Bydgoszcz. When Menno went to the camps to find people, the MCC workers would assemble packages to take along to give out. They packed a blanket, underwear and other clothes, and some food. So we took a package like this to my Aunt Wanda.

Going to that camp was very scary! Aunt Wanda and I were very happy to see each other, but we couldn't talk very much. I told her I was with MCC, and maybe they would help me reach Germany, but I asked her not to tell anybody who I was or why I visited her.

Aunt Wanda had an infected finger which she had wrapped in a cloth. And she told me that she was working for the government office in that camp. She asked if I knew anything about my mother. But since Menno didn't have my mother on a list, we didn't know if she was alive or dead.

Sometimes other people that Menno had found would come to the house for Sunday dinner. They would come on Sunday for a little church service and Sunday dinner and then for some visiting after dinner. Then Menno would take them back. The Dyck sisters, Helga and Gundela, were originally from West Prussia. There were also two other Mennonite girls who had come from Elbing. One of the girls from Elbing was a cook at a doctor's office in Pelplin. She thought life was pretty good there, so she didn't want to put her name on the list to emigrate.

Two different women named Mrs. Penner came to the house sometimes. One was a single lady in her 50s, who lived in Danzig. I think she must have been free already. She was living in a little suite, and I think she was pretty well educated.

The other Mrs. Penner had a daughter named Mrs. Pauls. Mrs. Pauls had a seven-year-old daughter, Lili, and a four-year-old son, Werner. Werner liked the canned peaches that came from America. He would eat them quickly and then ask for more. His mother said, "No son, you've had your share." But Rachel said, "It's all right, you can have some more." So Werner would eat some more and then say, "Now I've had enough."

After breakfast Yadja and I would clean off the table and begin the chores. We cleaned the house, cleaned the floors, washed the windows inside, and sometimes we cleaned the vegetables for dinner. Ruth Miller cooked the dinner, and sometimes we helped her.

Someone in the house would go to town once a week for groceries. I didn't go along all the time, but one time I went with Rachel to buy wool. We bought some green wool and I knitted in my spare time. I made myself a scarf and some mittens with that green wool.

After the evening meal, Mrs. Miller would clear the dishes from the table. But usually I said, "Don't worry about it. You cooked, let me clean the dishes." So I would wash the dishes. Then the MCC workers would sit around the table and plan what they would each do the next day – where they would take food and so forth. Since I didn't understand English very well and couldn't follow along, I often wondered how I would fill my evenings.

Sometimes after the evening meal, Menno gave me lessons in typing. He also taught me a few words and numbers in English, but I thought it was so hard to learn! There was a Polish lady who came to have tea with Rachel sometimes. She spoke English, and when she left I'd wonder, "How did this Polish woman learn English?" It made me want to learn English even more.

I had a bedroom all to myself upstairs. It was a small room with a single bed and plenty of blankets. My room was next to the Fishers' room. Sometimes Rachel would come into my room at night and sit on my bed to talk or pray before we went to sleep. Before I went to sleep each night I said the Lord's Prayer. That was the prayer that my Mom had taught me. I said it to myself very often during those difficult years after the war.

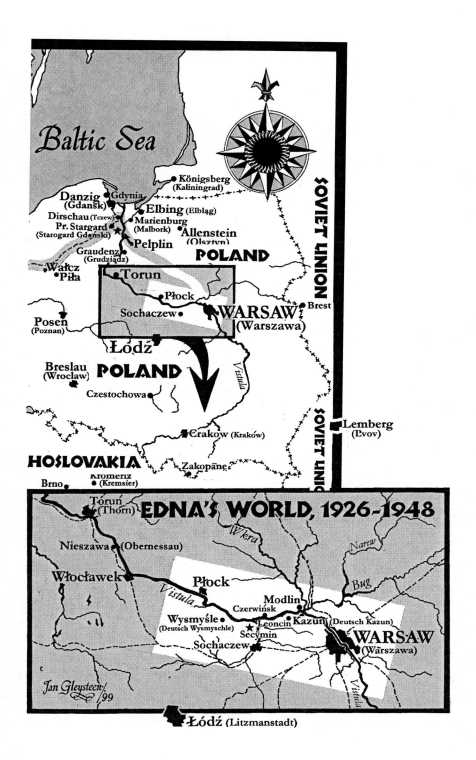

Baltic Sea

Königsberg
(Kaliningrad)

Danzig • Gdynia
(Gdansk)
Dirschau (Tczew)
Pr. Stargard
(Starogard Gdański)
Pelplin

Elbing (Elbląg)
Marienburg
(Malbork)
Allenstein
(Olsztyn)

Graudenz
(Grudziądz)
•Wałcz
•Piła

POLAND

Torun

Płock

Brest

Sochaczew •

WARSAW
(Warszawa)

Posen
(Poznan)

Łódź

Breslau
(Wroclaw)

POLAND

Vistula

Czestochowa•

Lemberg
(Lvov)

Crakow (Kraków)

HOSLOVAKIA

Zakopane

Brno•

Kromeriz
(Kremsier)

Torun
(Thorn)

EDNA'S WORLD, 1926-1948

Wkra

Narew

Nieszawa •(Obernessau)

Włocławek

Vistula

Płock

Bug

Modlin

Czerwińsk

Wysmyśle •
(Deutsch Wysmyschle)

Leoncin Kazuń (Deutsch Kazun)

Secymin

WARSAW
(Warszawa)

Sochaczew •

Vistula

Jan Gleysteen/
/99

Łódź (Litzmanstadt)

CH·7

MOONLIT CROSSING

One night, after I had been at Pelplin for a couple of months, I decided that I could never go back to the prison camps in Poland. I didn't know what I would do, but I knew I couldn't go back. That night, I cried and cried until I thought I had come to the end. I actually began to wish that death would come. That was when I realized I had to leave Poland for good.

The time had come for Rachel and Bob to leave the unit, and I was getting nervous. I knew the longer I was there, the greater chance there would be for someone to get suspicious. Rachel and Bob and Menno wanted to help me in whatever way they could. That's when we decided I would try to escape to Germany on foot.

When I left Pelplin that sixth of June, I had no idea what was ahead of me. I didn't know what to expect. But I just said, "Lord, here I am." Somehow it was so clear to me what I had to do. And I felt so strongly that it was the right thing. There was a voice in me that said, "Just go, just go."

The worst thing about leaving was having to say good-bye to the Fishers and the other MCC workers. They had become so important to me, and it was hard to let them go. I wasn't able to be close with any Polish people – I did not trust them, they had done so many bad things to me. But with the Fishers, it was different.

Menno said I should try to reach the refugee camp in Gronau, on the Western border of Germany. And he told me a little bit about what to expect in Gronau. He said there were Mennonites there. But I didn't have a picture of what it would be like. I just trusted him.

Rachel and Bob gave me some things before I left. I put on two of each garment, and I carried a little bag. In my bag I carried a little container of sewing needles, some chocolate, a little plastic folding cup for water, and a little knife. We opened up the fabric of the belt on my dress so I could hide my money inside. I wanted to keep it safe so that no one would steal it from me. When I needed some money, I would rip open that belt, take out some money, and then sew it shut again. I had to wear a pair of men's shoes because after all those years of going barefoot, my feet had grown kind of wide.

Each of the MCC workers received ten dollars a month for their expenses. That month, everyone in the house gave their ten dollars to me for my trip! So I had ninety dollars! I could not believe how nice they all were to me. They gave me their American dollars because they thought they would go farther than Polish zlotys. American dollars were very valuable in Europe at that time.

What has stayed in my mind until this very day is saying good-bye. It was so hard! I remember when I kissed Rachel good-bye at the train station, I said, "Lord, I may never see these people in Poland again, but even if it takes 50 years, I will see them again!" I could not take along their address or any other information, but I knew that I would find a way to see them again.

Menno Fast traveled with me for part of the way. We started by train in the evening, and arrived early in the morning in Szczecin. We did not encounter any problems on this part of the trip. Menno just showed his passport and said I was his friend or his sister.

We saw lots of Russian soldiers on the train – it was very scary. In Poland I didn't see so many, but on that train there were a lot of Russian soldiers. We didn't talk to each other on the way, Menno and I. We didn't want anyone to hear us speaking German.

We came to Szczecin, and I had the address of someone I knew there, someone who I thought would help me get out. I had the address memorized, and when we arrived in Szczecin, we walked to find it. When we got closer, I got a bit nervous about this. I wondered if the address was correct, and I wondered what would happen if my friend wasn't at home.

We found my friend's house on Marszałkowska Street. I asked the woman at the train station if she knew how to find that street, and she gave me directions. There was a little park close to my friend's house, and Menno said he would wait there to make sure everything was okay. He took a Polish newspaper that he had on the train, and pretended to read it. And he waited.

I walked up to the house and a lady came to the door. In Polish I said "Hello," and asked if I had the correct address. She looked at me rather strangely, like she didn't have any idea what I wanted. Then I gave her the name of my friend. "Yes," she said, "she lives here, but she has gone out." And she invited me in. She spoke German, but this wasn't unusual since Szczecin was once a German city (Stettin). She was my friend's housekeeper, I found out later.

The housekeeper let me in to wait until my friend came home. I remember she was doing the wash in a big bucket with a washboard. Her Polish was pretty broken, because she was a German who had stayed when Poland took over the area.

Meanwhile, Menno still waited outside in the park. I had told him that when I knew that everything was all right, I would come outside and give him a signal. I told the housekeeper I wanted to go outside and get some paper to write a letter to someone. There was a drugstore near the house, but I really just wanted to give Menno the signal that I was all right. I didn't tell the truth because I still didn't trust anybody. I was afraid that housekeeper might get suspicious and turn me in to the police.

She said I mustn't go outside. She was very worried that the neighbors would see me and wonder what was happening. I just looked through the window. I could see Menno sitting there, but I could not signal to him that I was okay.

After several hours it was time for his train to leave. He later told me that he simply prayed and gave me up into the Lord's hands. He had brought me as far as he could, it was time to let me go. I felt bad that he didn't know I was at the right place. But then I thought he knew that if I couldn't get help from that friend, I would cross the border by myself.[1]

My friend came home later, and she was surprised to see me! We talked for a while about what I should do. She told me that she had some relatives in Germany who helped to smuggle people over the border. She and her husband also helped smuggle bread into the Russian Zone of Germany, since there was more bread in Poland at that time. Then she said we would have to wait and talk to her husband about what to do with me.

My friend and I were very glad to see each other. We talked and talked. But I was afraid to say too much about my time in Danzig.

That was the way things were then. I was afraid she would accidentally say too much sometime, and then the MCC people would get in trouble. In the evening her husband came home and we talked things over. They were very friendly to me, they gave me a good supper and tea, and we visited.

They said the Polish and the Russians were sending a lot of people across the Oder River to Germany. My friend's husband said it would be very dangerous to try to cross the border, since it was so well guarded. Many people had been killed while trying to cross. But he said that we would try a way that was a little bit safer. He explained how they would smuggle me on a train which would cross the border, transporting German refugees with valid transit visas. Though I had no such visa, I could stay on the train until it crossed the border into the East Zone of Germany. They said I would be relatively safe up to the border. But then I would need to jump the train and then walk from there, finding my way by myself to Gronau as best I could. I would need to do all this alone, of course.

Then they said we needed money to pay the officer who was helping them smuggle people across. We sent a telegram to Pelplin and asked them to send us money. We needed 5,000 zlotys. That sounds like a lot of money, but after the war, the zloty was devalued so much that 1,000 zlotys was not very much money. I remember that a pair of shoes would cost from 3,000 to 5,000 zlotys.

I think I waited there a few days for the money before I could go. But I didn't wait very long. One morning there was a knock at the door. We opened it, and there was Cliff Kenagy, one of the MCC workers. He said, "Good morning," and he came in and we visited a while. He said he brought the money. Then I think in an hour or two his train left for Pelplin, and he was gone.

I gave the money to my friend's husband, and he told me I would have to wait in a camp where refugees were waiting to get on the train. So my friend walked the distance with me, but she left me before we reached the camp – she didn't want to be seen too close to it.

On the way to the camp, I passed a photographer who was trying to sell people pictures of themselves. He would take your picture, and in a few minutes give you a copy of it. I asked him how long it would take for the picture to be ready, and he said, "Only 15 minutes or so." So I thought that since I was getting ready to leave on this big adventure, and I had a little bit of Polish money left, I would have him take my picture. I still have that picture.

At the camp there was a large group of German refugees waiting to be taken back to Germany. I went up to the office window and gave the secretary my name. She had my name on some sort of list. We waited there for perhaps a day or two before we could board the train. I remember sleeping on the floor, waiting to leave. It was so crowded! At night, when people wanted to go to the washroom, they just climbed over sleeping bodies.

It was early afternoon when we finally left the station. The train traveled south, very close to the Oder River on the Polish side. The train was full of German refugees. The people were so poor, and so tired-looking. I must say I had on a nicer dress than most of the others. On the train there were benches facing each other, and at the end of the car were the washrooms.

People were sitting and standing everywhere in all the spaces not occupied by boxes or piles of blankets. It was so crowded that it soon got pretty warm. So they opened some of the windows to let the air in. Some people went to the washroom, some people slept a little bit, there were babies crying. Nobody was asking any questions or talking very much. Everyone was just waiting to cross over, out of Poland.

There were no soldiers or officers that I remember on the train. The conductors would sometimes walk back and forth in the cars and look a little bit, and then go back. It was pretty calm.

I was told that when we crossed the river, we would be in the Russian Zone of Germany. There was a stop just across the river, where the checkpoint was. I was supposed to jump off the train through the window before it stopped. They told me to look for a mill, and as soon as I saw it, I was supposed to jump. Here, instead of the usual whistle, the train's bell would also ring, longer than usual – a second signal that this was the moment to jump. It was only a kilometer or so from there to the station.

I remember the train was slowing down as it approached the station, and then the train bell began to clang very loudly – and there was the mill! It was evening when I jumped off the train. We had been traveling only a few hours. The light was fading, but I could still see a little bit. I had thought I would be the only one going over the border illegally, but I saw that there were about a half dozen or more other people who were also jumping off and immediately running into the forest.

I was so tired, and so nervous. I wasn't sure if I was out of Poland yet, but I assumed I was in the Russian Zone of Germany.

I threw my little bag first, and then I jumped. During the whole trip I was worrying about how I was going to jump off. I was afraid the train would be going too fast and the speed would throw me down too hard. But it was not going very fast. I could have been afraid, but I knew I just had to do it. I hurt my knee a little bit when I landed on the gravel, and I fell into some nettles on the side of the tracks which stung for awhile. Otherwise I was fine.

Then I had to go back for my bag. I thought, I cannot lose that, it has precious things in it. I walked a little farther and found it lying in the bushes. I grabbed it and started running through the woods. They had told us to run through the forest as far as we could. So I ran and ran. Finally I stopped and hid until morning. I was so tired! I found a little bush to hide behind, and I slept there all by myself. Soon it grew cold and I thought, what if a wolf comes? So I became frightened and started to walk.

I walked a little farther and then I saw a field with sheaves of oats and I thought, there I will make my nest and sleep. I don't know how long I slept – time was not time. The sun was different – was it morning? Was it evening? The directions were mixed up. But I did not care, I just wanted to sleep some more until I felt a little better.

I had seen people jumping off the train with me, but the woods and brush were so thick that everyone disappeared. They had told me when I left Pelplin that it would be much faster to walk straight to Gronau. But it was too dangerous. There were a lot of people who wanted to cross over into the American Zone. Even some people on the train said it would be so nice if they could go straight across the border. But they also said there were many places where people who tried to cross were shot or sent back to the camps. So I thought to myself that I should go towards the South. I knew it would take much longer, but I had all the time in the world, and I thought it would be safer.

As I walked on a path through the woods, I passed two ladies with shopping bags. They were speaking German to each other, so I knew I was in Germany. I could not understand all they were saying, but I heard them say something like, "If only we had a little salt, we could make turnip soup."

Soon I started seeing signs to Leipzig. I also saw signs to Berlin, lots of signs to Berlin. But I knew that Berlin was to the North, and Leipzig was to the South. I wanted to head towards Leipzig. I had been in Leipzig on my way home from the camp in Potsdam, so I knew it pretty well.

Most of the time I would sleep in sheaves of oats or barley, but haystacks were even nicer. In those sheaves I thought perhaps a dog would come, or closer to the forest maybe a wolf or a snake or even a mouse or a rat. When I would find a nice haystack I would climb up to the top, make a hole, climb in and put the hay back so that the haystack would look the same again. And there I slept very nicely. I could look up to the sky, and say a little prayer. Sometimes I would hear birds singing and I would think, Oh, I wish I could be a bird and just fly. It would be faster than walking. Then I would sleep again until I felt rested.

The most dangerous border I had to cross was between the Russian and American zones in Germany. I had counted on taking a train part of the way, but as it turned out, that was impossible. Menno thought my trip to Gronau would take me three days. But it took me three months! Menno often went back and forth to Holland, and Gronau wasn't very far from Holland. So he would stop in with his lists and find people and ask them about others who might still be in Poland. Menno came on the train that way, and he said it was one of the shortest trips he had taken. But it was very dangerous. He did not like going through the Russian Zone because they stopped him and went through all of his papers and things. He was afraid they would find out what he was doing. So the next time he went to Holland, he made an enormous detour past Krakow in southern Poland, and then west through Czechoslovakia and Austria.

But when he traveled through the Russian Zone he needed different money. So when I was ready to walk he gave me some of his leftover Russian money. He said that when I crossed into the Russian Zone, I would have more than three hundred kilometers before I would reach the American Zone. He told me to take the money and go to Leipzig, and buy a train ticket to the border. Then again I would have to sneak across the border on foot.

When I got to Leipzig, I knew where the train station was. I went to the counter and asked for a ticket to a town closer to the border. A very nice lady was behind the counter, and she looked at me a little funny and said, "I'm sorry Miss, but two days ago we changed currency. You can't use that old money anymore."

So I blushed a little, and hoped that she wouldn't ask me where I had come from. I was very frightened of being discovered, since I came over "schwarz" (illegally). So I simply said, "I'm sorry, I didn't know." So my money was useless! I think I carried it with me anyway until I reached Gronau.

Since I couldn't go by train, I walked. I had time, so I just did it. After talking to the ticket agent, I thought I should leave the city as quickly as I could. Leipzig was a fairly large city at that time. But before I left, I stopped at a little store.

There were several stores in Leipzig, and although they were also badly damaged from the bombing, you could find some things to buy. I went into one where a young woman was selling books and cards and a few other things. I thought I should buy myself a book with the American money I had hidden in my belt. I thought it would give me something to do, so I wouldn't be alone with my thoughts all the time. But I looked at the prices, and they were so expensive!

She also had some maps there, so I thought I'd buy a map to help me in my journey. And that's what I did. For the rest of the trip, I used that little map to guide me. When I saw signs to different places I would mark it on my map and try to figure out where I was and how much farther I had to go. I think I made pretty good time. I averaged about 35 kilometers a day.

As I was leaving Leipzig, a big truck full of turnips pulled up. People lined up all around the truck to get some turnips. They opened the end gate, and the turnips spilled all over the street. People had to show some papers to the soldiers – a ration card or something and then they would get their turnips. If there were three people in the family they got three turnips. And if there were seven, they got seven turnips. If the women didn't have bags to put them in, they would just carry them in their shirts, or in their shawls. I wished I could also have a turnip.

As I traveled, I stayed by myself the whole time. There were other refugees walking in the Russian Zone – more than in the American Zone. In the American Zone there was more to eat, but here the people had very little to eat. Everything was bombed out and people had nothing. The Russians were taking most of the food from this zone and transporting it back to Russia. And there was a lot of hunger. People wandered on the roads and in the towns, looking for food or looking for lost relatives. It was so hard. People were begging, but there was nothing to give.

Sometimes at night I would open my belt and take out money, hoping the next day to find some food that I could buy. One time I bought two tomatoes, another time a cucumber, and once I bought a loaf of bread from some ladies who were selling it on the black market (there was no bread at all in the stores or bakeries). One lady I passed whispered to me, "I have bread to sell, I have bread to sell." It looked pretty nice on top, and I thought to myself, "This will last a whole week."

I took my little knife to cut a piece of the bread but it did not cut. The bread was like clay, the knife blade was sticky. I don't know what they used to make the bread, but it was heavy like a rock in my stomach. I ate just a little at a time, and that bread lasted a long time – far longer than a week!

In Poland I didn't see many Russian soldiers, but here I saw them walking everywhere. That made me very scared. I could even smell them on the streets. They ate something strange, and they smelled like that food. And when they were finished eating, they didn't wash, they just wiped their hands on their clothes. So they looked and smelled dirty.

In July and August the harvest was already coming in. People would steal food from the fields. Sometimes the farmers would let them glean, like Ruth in the Bible did. And that helped me quite a bit too. I would blow the chaff away and then would have a handful of wheat to chew. It was something to do as I walked, and it gave me a little more strength. Some people carried sacks and collected food that they ate along the way. I didn't have a bag. I simply ate as I went along.

When I left Pelplin, the MCC people gave me some chocolate. I ate it little by little, dividing it so it would stretch over a long time. I would steal a little bit: some carrots, and fruit from the trees, and potatoes, and wild berries. I had some matches, so when I was deeper in the forest, I would take some dry twigs and make a fire. I learned how to do that in my school years. I baked potatoes in the fire.

In some towns there were Red Cross kitchens. I came to several of these accidentally. There were so many people in Germany after the war who needed help. There were Jews and Poles, and Czechs who had survived the war and now were trying to find work on their own. Everybody was walking – trying to find relatives or jobs. The Red Cross was very helpful for refugees. They helped people find their families, and gave them food. They had set up soup kitchens where they gave out soup and a piece of bread. So I went to those whenever I found them.

Sometimes we refugees would talk to one another. We would tell each other where the next kitchen was, and how far we planned to go and how many days it would take. There were so many people walking! There were also many people from Germany itself. I met many people who had lived in Dresden and who lost their homes when the Americans and the British bombed Dresden so badly.

I kept moving. I never stayed in one town for more than a day. There was nothing to eat in the more populated areas, and there was more danger of running into Russians. Usually I could find some potatoes or something to eat in the fields. There were so many forests in Germany, I could hide in the forest and nobody would know that I was there. When I was deep enough in the woods, I could make a little fire with some dried leaves or twigs and cook my food. And then I would lie back and watch the fire and rest.

Menno had given me a little cup for drinking. There was usually enough rainwater in ditches around for washing my hands and face, and for drinking. And amazingly, I never got sick from drinking it. When I cooked my potatoes, I often cooked three or four at a time. I would eat one, and put the others in my bag and have them the next day. And I picked carrots too. I know it was stealing, but I never took more than I could eat. Sometimes I would take an extra one or two for the evening or the next day, but no more than that.

Since it was summer time, there were berries and fruit to be eaten along the way. Ever since I can remember, food was not the number one concern for me. I could go without food. One needs a little bit to stay alive, but I must say that hunger wasn't the hardest part for me. The constant fear of being caught was much harder to bear.

I enjoyed seeing the countryside as I walked. The land was pretty hilly, with small farms and sheep in the pastures. It was more beautiful to me than Poland. In Poland there were more trees, but here there were rolling pastures. I would almost look forward to each day, wondering what I would see next.

The time that I was walking became all tangled up for me. Telling the story now, I can't remember how many days I spent walking. Day and night blended together. Sometimes I would be walking, and I would get mixed up about which direction I was going. But then I would watch the sun, and if it got higher and higher, I knew it was morning. Some days I would walk for a long time – I just kept walking. And other days I needed more sleep, so I would rest longer. I never knew if it was Monday or Saturday, or what month it was. Time seemed to stretch on and on.

I traveled on roads sometimes, but mostly on smaller paths. Roads led from one town to the next, but there was a lot of traffic and soldiers on the roads. Perhaps they wouldn't have done anything to me, but I was scared. I was scared of all men, soldiers and civilians. So I stayed away from most people. I didn't talk very much or ask questions.

One time, though, as I was coming closer to the border between the Russian and American zones, I came upon an old couple. They were in their field, raking hay. They had two goats. They looked at me and asked, "You are a refugee too?" And I said, "yes." Then they asked, "Do you want to go over the border?" Oh, then I wondered if I should tell them. Maybe they were spies. But finally I said, "Yes, I would love to." They said, "Just go a little farther and you will see a tower for the power lines. Go from one transmission tower to the next, they will lead you across the border." So that's what I did.

It was night time then. The moon shone brightly, so I could see a little bit. I walked from one tower to another. Sometimes I couldn't see the next tower, but I walked anyway, and pretty soon I would see it. They were pretty far apart. The moon would go behind a cloud and then I couldn't see anymore. So I would wait for the clouds to part, and then I would walk again.

I had two pretty bad scares at this time. I was usually scared, but these two experiences stayed with me. As I was trying to locate the next tower in the woods, I came to a low place where the ground was soft. I knew I dared not lose track of the transmission towers, but I was having a hard time walking. It was a bog, where the ground is really soft and underneath is water. The ground was so spongy. I was so afraid that I would sink in and not be able to get out. There I was by myself, in this swamp, my legs sinking in, and nobody knew I was there! Nobody. But somehow I made it through.

The couple had also told me to be careful for another reason. The checkpoint for crossing the border was about three kilometers away from where I would cross. So there could be a lot of soldiers in the area. I remember hearing dogs barking in the distance, and not knowing if they were getting closer or not.

For a while I walked near a roadway that curved and wound around the hillside. Everything was quiet except for the dogs barking. But all of a sudden I saw the reflection of a light and heard a motor approaching. I thought, "Now I will certainly get caught!" I knew I had to hide quickly. The lights came up over a hill maybe a quarter of a kilometer away, and then disappeared. Then the lights came back over the next hill towards me.

There weren't very many trees in the area, but there was one little evergreen tree. I've often said that the Lord put that tree there just for me. Very quickly I threw my bag behind the tree, and swung myself around to the other side, right before the motorcycle passed, not even ten feet away. As I peeked out, I saw that the driver had a big rifle on his back. So I thought for sure he was a soldier who was patrolling the border.

It was a little hilly there, and the forest was thick. After the motorcycle passed I decided to stay close to the road but not on it. And that's the way I came across. I must have walked close to 35 kilometers that night. Fear was pushing me faster and faster. I knew that if I could cross this border, I would be safe.

The next day I knew I had made it across. I could tell by looking at the map I had bought in Leipzig that I had crossed the Russian border. I felt like I was in the Old Testament, when they would build an altar to the Lord after he had brought them safely to another place. I was so thankful, I knew that I had made it. I was out of danger! I hid again behind some snow fences, and there I could rest and pray. I prayed and cried tears of joy because I was so happy. In Poland I had been given a small New Testament with Psalms, and so I read my favorite Psalm: the Twenty-Third. That was my altar to the Lord, where I uttered my heart-felt thanks and gratitude to God. Surely and truly, the borders were, thanks be to God, now behind me!

Sometimes my grandchildren ask me how I could walk so far. But you know, we were used to it back then. And walking was one thing I missed when I came here to Canada. Back in Europe we walked everywhere. We rode bicycles, too, but mostly we walked. During the War we walked quite a bit. And afterwards, when I was in those prison camps, we walked everywhere.

In the American Zone I felt safe. It was a very different feeling. I didn't know how far away Gronau was, or how long it would take me to get there. But the worst was over, that I knew. The most dangerous, scary part was finished.

I kept walking until I reached Bamberg. I remember I was so hungry, so I went to a restaurant to see if they had anything to eat. I told them I was a refugee and I didn't have much money, but I would be grateful for just a little soup or something. They said, "We're sorry, it's after lunchtime, and we have nothing left over." But the woman said, "I could give you some beer."

I was just north of Bavaria now, where the people drank more beer than coffee or tea or water. I had never tasted beer before in my life, but I thought, "Well, I will drink beer." She brought me a glass to a table where I was sitting in a corner. The glass was so nice and big, and the beer was all foamy. So I took a sip. But it was so bitter! I couldn't believe how bitter it was, it made my whole mouth taste bitter. I knew I couldn't drink it all. Besides, I knew that beer and Schnapps made you drunk, and I didn't want to be drunk.

So I looked around for somebody – I was going to say thank you and just leave. But I couldn't find anybody. It was all quiet, perhaps someone was back in the kitchen, but I couldn't see anyone.

So I got up and left, with the beer still sitting on the table, and I didn't even say thank you!

This was in the American Zone, but still there was not much to eat. And there were so many refugees. Mothers were walking with their children held close, just looking for somewhere to go and something to do. At night they perhaps had shelter, but during the day they just walked around looking for help. I don't know where everyone found food. The cities were all bombed out, so the refugees often went out to the farms and villages to try to find more to eat than was in the cities. And this was a couple of years after the war was over! But there still wasn't enough for everyone.

When I was still in Europe I was used to having so many people around. But when I came to Saskatchewan, at first I thought, "Where are all the people?" I was a bit lonely. In Europe people were everywhere, walking on the streets. I thought for sure I was in a different country when I came to Canada!

I spent a few days in Bamberg. By that time I was pretty worn out. I had been walking barefoot most of the time, I carried my shoes so they would last a little longer – maybe even be good enough to take to North America, I hoped. I had not been sleeping properly, and sometimes I was too cold, and sometimes I was too hot. So this had really worn me out.

In Bamberg there was an inn, or guest house, where they would give out their leftovers to the refugees after meals. I got food there a couple of times. One time I met a woman who lived in the yard of the hotel. She did the washing for the hotel and for others in town, and she was really friendly to me. She asked me where I was going and where I came from. I told her I was trying to get to Gronau.

"Oh," she said, "you have quite a ways to go yet."

Then the woman looked at my feet and said, "And your feet, you must have gone quite a ways already!"

My feet were swollen and rough with wounds and scratches coming from having walked in so many forests. My soles had long become toughened and I was accustomed to walking barefoot on streets and paths, even gravel, without minding it.

This woman also was a refugee who had come from Elbing, near Danzig. She had two little children, and her husband had been killed in Russia. On the trip her children had died – from malnutrition, or from the cold or something. She was perhaps ten years older than I was. We quickly became friends.

Then she said I looked tired, and asked if I wanted to stay and rest a little bit. I said, "Where will I stay? I'd better keep going until I get to Gronau."

"You can stay with me," she said.

In that little house she had one room with a bed and a chair and a few belongings. And she said, "I am making a little money here, so I will stay until I can afford to move on and try to find some relatives." So she let me stay with her for a few nights. She even gave me her bed to sleep in.

I think we understood each other pretty well. She had nothing and I had nothing. She was a refugee and I was a refugee. So we could talk to each other. She was kind of settled there in Bamberg, with her job and her little room. One day this washerwoman asked me, "What relatives do you have in Gronau?" In the beginning I didn't like to tell her everything, but eventually I knew I could trust her. So I told her that I had an uncle in Gronau.

I had found this out from Menno Fast back in the MCC Unit at Rolin, Pelplin. When Menno had earlier traveled to Gronau for a conference, he discovered that I had an uncle who was living close to Gronau. Menno had all kinds of lists, and was always trying to help people find their relatives. He found out it was my Uncle Peter – my father's youngest brother – and Aunt Florence. They were refugees too, and had first gone to Gronau, but he had gotten work on a farm nearby. So they were living close to the camp.

Uncle Peter had been a soldier for Germany, and was in a prison in the American Zone after the war. My Aunt Florence came on the trek from Warsaw when many people fled towards Germany in front of the advancing Russians. They came close to Leipzig too. I forget how they crossed the border. She told me, but I've forgotten. She came to Gronau first, before my uncle. And through the Red Cross or MCC, they found each other.

When the washerwoman found out I had an uncle living near Gronau, she said: "Oh, why don't you just send him a telegram and ask him to send you money for the train?"

"But how long will that take?" I asked. "I can't stay here in Bamberg too long to wait for it." But she said, "It will only take a few days, and you can stay here with me."

Then she told me I should go to the forest and look for mushrooms for the restaurant at the inn. I was used to picking mushrooms. Before the war when I was still at home, there was a forest pretty close to our village, and my sister and I would go into the woods and bring back mushrooms to eat. Sometimes the forest people would come into our village, too, and sell mushrooms that they had picked in the forest.

I knew that the best time to pick mushrooms was in the morning after a rain. When it's too hot or too dry, they don't grow. So the next morning I got up early. It was raining a little bit, and I didn't want to waste any time. I went to the kitchen and asked for a basket to put the mushrooms in.

I found so many mushrooms! It was like they were growing just so I could pick them. I found a patch here under this tree, and there under another tree. Before too long my basket was totally full. The people at the restaurant could hardly believe it. I said, Yes, there were even more – if they would want, I could go and pick some more.

They were so nice to me then. They said I could come back at lunchtime and they would give me something to eat. The washer woman also gave me some things to eat. She had some pears and some nice, red tomatoes, and some bread, which we ate together.

After we ate she said, "Now I will help you." She spoke German better than I did, and knew how to do things. I didn't even know we could send a telegram from the train station! So she went with me, showed me how to do it, and paid for it herself!

We sent the telegram, and maybe two days later we received word that my ticket to Gronau was paid for! Before my departure, the washer-woman ran quickly into the bakery, came out with two rolls, a tomato and an apple. That was my lunch for the day. She put it in a bag and then told me that after Nuremberg, I was to take the D-Zug – the express train. After tearful good-byes, she put me on a bus to the train station. I took the train from Bamberg to Nuremberg, where I caught another express train. This train went to Frankfurt, where I had to take a third train.

In Frankfurt, the train station was still heavily damaged from the war. There were deep holes where the bombs had hit, and there were boards across the holes, so people could walk across. The planks weren't very wide, so they let only one person at a time go across. But there were very many people, and they were all in a hurry, so sometimes more people would push onto the plank, and it would swing a bit.

I thought, "Oh, I made it this whole way, and now I'm going to fall into that hole!" It was really deep, I certainly would have gotten hurt if I had fallen.

From Frankfurt I traveled to Münster on an express train, and from Münster I took a local train to Gronau. I think the whole trip was made out on one ticket. But it took a long time. I left Bamberg a little before noon and I arrived the next day at about 3 or 4 o'clock in the afternoon. So I traveled all through the night.

I had started out on my trek from Poland, leaving the MCC unit on June 6. Once I was in the Russian Zone, I walked 35 kilometers a day on average, or, when I came closer to the border, 35 kilometers a night. I arrived in Gronau three months later, September 9, 1948, after having traveled nearly 1,700 kilometers.

For many years afterwards, the washer-woman from Bamberg and I exchanged letters. And when I came to Canada and got a little settled, I wanted to send her some money or something. So I sent her airmail letters, and I enclosed some nylon stockings. They were not for her to wear, but to sell, to make a little money. For many years we wrote a couple times a year. But as the years went by, the time got longer and longer between letters. And finally I wrote a letter and got no reply, so I gave up too.

That was the first time I learned that you could send telegrams. Someone must have taken the message from the train by bike or by foot to my uncle on the farm and told him that he had a niece in Bamberg who needed money. And he just went to the train station in Gronau and paid for the ticket there.

It wasn't easy for him, I'm sure. The ticket may have cost him at least a week's salary, and he had three children to take care of. For a long time after that I asked him if I could repay the price of the ticket. But he said, "No, Edna. That was the only thing I could do to help you."

Notes:

[1] Menno Fast, in his occasional journal, entered his own account of those events leading up to Edna's departure from Poland (see the excerpt for June 5-8, 1948, published below in the Documents section).

CH•8

"ERHOLUNG"

The train arrived in Gronau in the early evening of September 9, 1948, and I walked the two or three kilometers from the station to the farm where my Uncle Peter worked. I guess I must have asked someone for directions, otherwise I wouldn't have known how to find my way.

I stayed with Uncle Peter and Aunt Florence for a day or two. After we shared some of our experiences, I thanked them for their generosity, and set out for the MCC refugee camp.

As I approached the gates outside the camp, I started feeling afraid of what would happen, since I didn't have any papers. I found out that the camp was only for refugees. Many people wanted to get papers to emigrate to America and Canada – even Germans whose homes were near Gronau. But MCC was only supposed to work with people who had no place to go, so they had to watch carefully who came and went. Menno Fast had given me the names of Peter Dyck and Siegfried Janzen, so I told the people at the gate that they were the ones I wanted to see.

The guards took me to the office right away, where I had to fill out some papers. The secretaries in the office asked me where I had come from and if I wanted to stay in Germany or if I wanted to emigrate. I told them that since I had an uncle in Canada and another one in the States, I wanted to emigrate. They had lists: lists of names that people in North America had sent in, of relatives in Europe that they wanted to find. MCC workers then tried to locate the Europeans. I guess my uncle in Philadelphia and my uncle in Saskatchewan had both put my family's names on the list. The secretaries asked me where I wanted to go, whether I wanted to join my uncle in Philadelphia or my uncle in Saskatchewan. I said Saskatchewan. I was not a city girl. I was used to living on a farm, and I thought it would be easier for me to adjust to life there.

Gronau was a large camp with many different buildings.

Clubhaus was close to the villa where the MCC offices were, *Schitzenhof* was maybe a kilometer away, and *Eppe* was even a little farther away, in a different village.

After this first interview, they sent me to the building where I would sleep for the night. They told me that Clubhaus, the closest building, was full. So I had to go to Schitzenhof, which was a little farther away. I went there with a little slip of paper, saying that I had been to the office, and it was all right for them to let me in.

Schitzenhof was an old theater that MCC had cleaned out and filled with bunk beds. They hung blankets from the ceiling to divide the large room into smaller rooms, and then they put beds in these "rooms." Sometimes there were two beds to a room, and sometimes four. It wasn't fancy, but at least we had a little room to sleep.

The kitchen was also in Schitzenhof. We ate at long tables stretched across a big room. The building was much bigger than the MCC house in Poland. There were so many people at Gronau! I would guess that there were 700 or 800 people there at a time. I wondered from where they had all come! Almost all the people at Gronau were Mennonite refugees.

Some people who had been staying in Schitzenhof had just left for Canada, so there were lots of empty beds. The beds didn't have mattresses, there was just a little straw, or straw bags. We each had two blankets – army blankets – and that was all. Those were our sleeping quarters. But it was a nice big building, and we could bathe there too.

The young man who gave me my blankets that first night was also a refugee. They gave all the refugees work assignments, so we would have something to do while we waited for our papers to come through. The young man's name was Jacob Dyck and he eventually came to Canada too. For forty years he was our neighbor here in Saskatchewan!

The camp was very well organized. It was such a good thing to be able to work! It was a camp, but not at all like the other camps where I had been. We lived a very nice life there in Gronau.

A day or two after I arrived, I had to have a medical examination. They wanted to check everybody for diseases like tuberculosis, which was very common. They also checked for sexually transmitted diseases, or "Frauen sicknesses," which were common because of all the rape that happened. There was a hospital close to the camp, and the examination was the first thing I had to undergo while I was there.

As part of the examination, they drew my blood. I guess my blood was not in good condition after those months of not eating very well. So they sent me to the *Erholungsheim*, which was part of the refugee camp, but was a building just for the sick people. They called the time we spent there our *Erholung* time, our time of convalescence.

The Erholungsheim was right on the border of Germany and Holland. Inside the building there was a long hallway, and when you stood at one end of the hallway you were in Germany, and at the other end you were in Holland!

During my Erholung time I rested and ate, slept, read books and had time for Bible study. It was a time just for recuperation. But I soon became restless. I thought, "Here I am in Germany, I should be doing something." But they told me I should be patient and get healthy first.

In the beginning I was hungry all the time. I would eat my whole meal and get up from the table, and even though I was full I felt like I could still eat. But they couldn't feed us too much. It wouldn't have been good for us, and besides, they didn't have enough to feed everyone huge portions. So our portions were modest, but in the Erholungsheim they fed us more often. In between meals we ate apples and other things to help build up our strength.

I had lost so much weight during my trip – when I first came to Gronau I weighed just under 100 pounds! I had gained weight while I was at the MCC house in Pelplin. Mrs. Miller prepared such good food that I even became a little bit round. But I lost all that extra weight while I was walking, since I didn't have much to eat. Even when there was food, the fear kept me from eating very much.

As was the practice at Gronau, I stayed in the Erholungsheim for a month. They kept a close watch on my blood and my weight. I was supposed to get plenty of sleep, but this was very hard for me then. I had such terrible nightmares! I often awoke in the night with a start. That kept up for many years.

I was restless. Finally I told Peter Dyck that I wanted to work.

I thought at least I could wash dishes or peel potatoes or something. The truth was that I wanted to be around more people. But Peter said, "just wait until you've regained your strength. Then you can work all you want."

Before I left Pelplin, Rachel had given me some good clothing, a couple of dresses and stockings and a towel and a sweater. She said to me, "Edna, you can have them. You don't have a sweater, and you will need one." I had plenty of clothes, but I couldn't carry them all with me. It would have been too difficult, and I didn't want to look like a refugee, since I had to sneak across the border. So when I left, I wore two dresses: one on top of the other. When it got too warm I took the bottom one off and put it in my bag and just wore the top one, which was gray. The bottom one was light green, and I thought, "How will I wash it if it gets dirty?" So I wore the gray one on top. For three months I wore that dress. I never took it off, I walked in it, slept in it and never washed it. And I still have that dress!

Menno told me that soon after I left Pelplin he would have to go to Brussels for a conference. So he packed my clothes in a suitcase and dropped them off at Gronau for me. He thought I would already be there by the time he passed through. I thought, "My, you are going the second mile for me!"

I knew it would be so nice to have those extra clothes. When Menno came to Gronau, he asked Elfrieda Dyck if I had arrived. But I hadn't, of course. So he gave the clothes to Elfrieda to keep for me.

When I went to Pelplin, I had given Rachel and Bob my real name, Edna. I didn't think I needed to say Yrcka or Erna which was what the Polish people called me. So Menno told the people at Gronau that an Edna Schroeder would be coming, and they should be expecting me. But instead of three days, I arrived three months later! And when I got there, there were the clothes from Rachel, waiting for me. But they weren't in the same suitcase. They were just in a box. I guess the suitcase had belonged to Menno, and he still needed it. These days we can just go to the store and buy a new suitcase, but in Europe at that time things were not so easy.

When I arrived and told them my name, Elfrieda asked if I was the Edna that Menno Fast had told her about. Then she asked me to follow her up to the attic above the office, and showed me the box of clothes she had saved for me. I was so glad I could change clothes and wash my dirty ones. I felt like I was starting a life that was almost normal![1]

I kept finding out what a small world it is. In the Erholungsheim, I found Heinrich Bartel and his wife – the same couple I had come upon in the shack when I was collecting signatures. They were staying in the same building I was in! We were so happy to have found each other.

Later on I helped them a bit. We washed our clothes by hand in the basement. Mrs. Bartel said she wanted to wash but she was so weak. She said she at least wanted to rinse her clothes so they wouldn't smell so bad. So I offered to wash their clothes for them. But I was also pretty weak. I worked up quite a sweat just washing the clothes! But I thought it was the least I could do. Before long, they went with the transport to Paraguay. They could not come to Canada or the States because they had a daughter who was sick. She had some type of sore on her leg that wouldn't heal, and you had to be very healthy to get permission to come to Canada or the States. So they went with Elfrieda Dyck on the ship the *Volendam* to Paraguay.

For a few years thereafter the Bartels and I wrote letters back and forth, up to the time of their deaths. Their daughter Frieda lived in Paraguay with them, but I never heard from her after they died. They had two daughters: Frieda, who was somewhat of a sickly child, and another daughter named Lydia. During the war the whole family had been separated, and afterwards they never found the other daughter.

Mrs. Bartel cried a lot over that lost daughter. She carried that sadness with her always. She said, "Now we have our freedom, and a place to stay and food to eat, but if only we could find Lydia!" They worked with MCC and the Red Cross to find her, but they didn't have any luck. The Bartels also had another child, a son, who had died in Russia in the war.

After I had spent about a month in the Erholungsheim, Elfrieda Dyck said they would find something for me to do. There was a girl doing the job that I eventually came to do, which was working as a telephone operator, putting through the calls that came from Switzerland and Austria and other places. This girl was kind of shy and very small, and her German was kind of bad, worse than mine. She was used to Polish and Ukrainian.

Her papers were ready to go to Canada, so Elfrieda said that when I felt ready I could learn to do her job. Even though I wanted a job so badly, I wasn't so sure I wanted that job. I thought it would be better for me to work with my hands instead of my head. I was pretty shy too, and I thought I needed some time to build up my courage. But she said they would give me two weeks to learn from the girl, and then she would be leaving for Canada.

The first week I made a lot of mistakes. Fräulein Lois Yake was the secretary there, and sometimes she would run down the stairs and say, "Fräulein Schroeder, you have made a mistake!" But when you mess up, you pay closer attention the next time. So after a while I learned what to do, and I even started to enjoy it very much.

Eventually, I was even a little sad that I had to quit that job. I enjoyed working with those people so much! I became friends with other girls in the office. One was Walli Ossenkopf (maiden name, Dyck), who eventually settled in Manitoba. We recently visited each other after all these years! We hardly recognized each other. She was a good writer. I think she came to Germany much earlier than I did – as early as 1945, perhaps. While I was in those camps in Poland, she was in school learning how to write. She learned shorthand and how to type, so she did her work very well.

Another friend whom I met in Gronau was Milda Rosener – she and I were such good friends! I was so happy to finally have friends and people I could trust. Milda went to join her uncle in British Columbia, and we have visited each other sometimes over the years.

Fräulein Yake was very busy. She had to prepare the papers for hundreds of people, so she had an assistant. Phone calls would come from Switzerland or Holland, and from the other MCC camps, like Krefeld. Our camp, Gronau, had been set up for the most part to prepare people for emigration. But I think at Krefeld they were doing more with rehabilitation: nursing people back to health and finding them jobs and getting them settled in Germany.

Peter Dyck and Siegfried Janzen worked in offices on the opposite side of the building from where I worked. There was a kitchen near their offices, and some other refugee girls worked there in the kitchen. On Easter the kitchen baked zwieback for us. I think Peter Dyck and the others liked to cheer us up by holding special events. They used celebration to help us recover from our time in the prison camps. So they arranged a ball game for the young people, and at least 300 people came! After the game these wagons rolled out, and the MCC workers served us zwieback and coffee from big kettles.

We also played "Dritten Abschlag," which involved people standing as couples in a circle – a boy and a girl together. One couple would run around, one trying to catch the other. The person being chased would grab hold of one side of a couple standing, and the person on the other side would then become the one being chased. Sometimes when we were running, we would fall down. That was pretty funny, because we girls wore dresses! In those years women didn't wear pants.

On Easter Monday the MCC workers invited us office girls to come for a little party with them. That was so nice! They served cake and coffee, and the men brought the cake around and served us. We refugee girls felt so special then – being served by MCC workers from America! We felt that they were so far above us, and we were just refugee girls, but we were treated so royally.

After they served us, the workers sat down and someone played the piano while we sang. Then Peter Dyck said, "Now I will tell you how I met my lovely wife." His wife Elfrieda was ten or so years older than I was. They were such a nice couple and it was a very interesting story, I'll never forget it. They had met in England during the war, while they were both doing volunteer work there. She was working as a nurse. He proposed to her while they were in a basement, with bombs falling all around them. I thought, "Oh, I would have other things on my mind than marriage with bombs falling around me!"

That little celebration and storytelling brought us a little bit closer together, and I think that helped us do our jobs better too. I felt close to them, but in a work kind of way. The Fishers and Menno Fast still felt more like family to me.

I worked closely with the whole staff there, and we spent most of our time trying to get the refugee people out. We tried to do the best we could to help people find their family members, and to emigrate. We worked with emigration officials and helped people get their papers and other things ready for the emigration process.

There continued to be up to 700 people at the refugee camp in Gronau at this time.

They took good care of us in Gronau. Even though we were refugees, they treated us with respect and kindness. If they saw that we needed clothes or shoes, they would give us some.[2]

I remember one time Elfrieda took me to the attic where they kept their clothes. She said, "Edna, I guess your shoes are pretty worn. We should find you some new ones." I thought, "Who cares? As long as I have shoes!" But she said that since I was working in the office I should wear decent clothes. And that was fine with me. The problem was that I had such big feet. The Schroeders all had pretty big feet. So it was hard to find a pair that fit.

Often the dresses and other clothes were very small. So Elfrieda would take two dresses, maybe a blue and a black one, and then we would open one up and sew panels from one dress into the other one to make it larger. Nearly everyone there knew how to sew.[3]

One of the nicest things about Gronau was the Baptist Church. There were three preachers at that church, and there was a wonderful big choir. A little later I joined the choir too. Every Friday the preacher's family came and sang songs with a guitar. There were about seven or eight of them, and they sang the nicest songs! I think their last name was Peters. They did it just to help us out. To give us food for the soul.

We would sit and listen, and sometimes sing along. Some of the songs were ones I didn't know, but many of them were ones my grandparents had sung, like "Welch' ein Freund ist unser Jesus," and others. Good old hymns. We wanted that family to come every evening!

One Sunday, before a ship left for Paraguay with refugees on board, there was a service in which there were ten weddings! They fed everyone zwieback and coffee. That was lunch for us. All the refugees were invited to that wedding in the villa. We sat outside on benches and chairs, and we celebrated.

One of the first Sundays that I was at Gronau, I sat in the church pew and listened to the call to come forward and be baptized. I thought that I would just stand up and go right then. But I hesitated – I knew I was not ready. I should prepare my heart first. But I didn't know how to do it.

Then one Sunday as I walked away from the church after the service, Cornelius Wall and his wife were walking behind me. I had to go back to the camp, and they had to go across the street to the villa where they were staying, where the MCC office was. Mr. Wall called out to me, "Fräulein Schroeder, wie geht's?" "I m okay," I said. And he must have seen on my face or something that I was not quite okay.

Then his wife said, "Would you like to come in the afternoon and have a cup of tea with us?" The Walls were living upstairs from the offices, they had their sleeping quarters upstairs. It was such a nice big building. The hospital was across the street, in another big building. The wealthy Dutch Mennonites were leasing the buildings to MCC, so that the staff members could live and work there.

So I told the Walls I would come that afternoon for tea. At tea, we started to talk, and they asked me questions to get to know me a little better. Cornelius asked me if I belonged to a church, and I said that my parents did but I did not, since I was a child when the war broke out. I hadn't gone to church for at least nine years or so. He asked if I wanted to be a member of a church. And I said I would love to be, but I was not quite ready yet.

He asked what was holding me back. "Lots of things," I said. When I came out of Poland, there were many stories of things that weren't quite straight. The thing that stood out in my mind was the time when I lied to the family in Warsaw, when I told them I would be coming back in three days, and I never went back. That was a difficult decision to make – whether to get Polish citizenship or to go with Bob and try to get out of Poland in a sneaky way. So I agonized over the fact that I had lied to that family.

I didn't feel right about it, and I knew I couldn't be baptized until I had dealt with it, until my heart was clean. But I couldn't deal with it by myself. I needed to get it off my chest and tell someone. So when I told the Walls that I had some things I needed to deal with first, Cornelius said, "Well, why don't we just talk it through, and see if we can help you with it." So I told him I was a liar. And he told me that I could bring things like that before the Lord and ask for forgiveness. I didn't even know I could do that! And then we prayed together, and I told them it was so hard for me, remembering the wrong things I had done. Sometimes I would lie awake at night and just cry, thinking about those things.

And he told me what Scripture says about Jesus taking sins that are red as scarlet, and washing them white as snow. He had it in German so I could read it. So we knelt down in prayer and asked the Lord to forgive me of the things I had done. And I felt them rolling off of me, like a heavy weight lifted. And I knew that they were really gone.

Cornelius told me that when I had things that I needed to talk about and get rid of, I should come back and we could talk through them. And I did go back and we spent many good hours together. Finally I felt I could really be happy inside. I was not yet ready to share the depth of my wartime and prison experiences with others, which in any case I had by no means sorted out. That would take me decades, and then, only in part. Even so, I felt at that moment that God had really forgiven me. So I was ready to be baptized. I was baptized with the next group on a Sunday morning, in the Baptist Church.

Our church services were held in a theater where on other nights they had shows. MCC rented it for Sunday. The young people would take the chairs and rearrange them in more of a church fashion. Some mornings we would come in and the place would still smell so bad – like cigarettes and beer, from the parties the night before. But the owners were kind enough to rent it for the church service. And all the refugees could fit in that building for worship.

But since the theater didn't have a place to do the baptisms, this service was held in the Baptist Church in Gronau. We had a class beforehand that Siegfried Janzen and Peter Dyck taught. They asked us questions, and we studied the Bible together. They asked how we came to the Lord and why we wanted to be baptized. The Sunday before we were baptized we each had to give our testimony in front of the church. Then the congregation asked us questions, and we answered as best we could. And then they would say that we were ready for baptism.

I was baptized on the 12th of June, 1949. All the people who were baptized that day were in the same class. Since we were with the Mennonite Brethren Church, we were dunked under the water, rather than "sprinkled." The pastor tipped us backwards in the water. Siegfried Janzen and Peter Dyck were both members of the General

Conference Church, and Cornelius Wall was part of the Mennonite Brethren Church. But Cornelius was too old to go in the water and tip people back, so Siegfried and Peter did most of the baptizing.

Everyone who was being baptized wore white. The outfits belonged to the Baptist Church. Everyone looked so nice, and the singing sounded so good – I thought I was in heaven!

Afterwards they gave us our baptism papers. "Finally!" I thought, "I have papers to show my identity." I didn't have a birth certificate, I didn't have a passport, but I had one piece of paper showing who I was and where I belonged. I was now a member of the church.

My good friend Milda Rosener had already been baptized. She was so nice to me! But I wondered why she never talked to me about being saved or getting baptized. I kind of wished that she would tell me what it was like. On the day I was baptized, we were walking back from the church, and I asked her, "Why don't you ever talk to me about God?" She said, "Edna, I thought you were already a Christian!"

Milda had a couple of sisters at Gronau. They were so nice too. And her mother always said to me, "Edna, come for coffee. I have three girls, but I can take you for my daughter too!"

For a while after I came to Canada, I kept in touch with some of my friends from Gronau. Milda was my best friend there, but I also kept in touch with Elsie Penner, who came to Winnipeg. Heda Rempel was another one of my friends. She slept in the bunk below me. She was very nice, too. But she went to Paraguay, and I never heard from her after that.

I stayed in Gronau for one whole year. That's how long it took to get my papers ready so I could come to Canada. Peter Dyck and Siegfried Janzen were working on it for me. I think they had some trouble since I came over the border illegally. I didn't have any papers, so they had to start from scratch. But they never told me what troubles they were having. I think they didn't want me to worry about it.

I know my case was also more difficult since I came over so late. During the first year or two after the war, so many people were crossing borders that it was pretty normal for people to come without papers. But since I came so much later, I think they had trouble because the governments were worried about spies.

It was very important to be healthy. The Canadian and American officials would only allow people who were really healthy to emigrate. So we had to pass several examinations. Many people had tuberculosis, or were sick from being malnourished for so long. I remember this caused so much sadness for some people! There were whole families who were trying to leave, and they would find that one person had trouble with his or her lungs – black spots on the lungs. So what would they do then? They couldn't leave that person behind, so none of them would go. The medical officials would tell them that they had to wait three months or nine months, or even longer, so that the person could get healthy. But that was so hard, just waiting and waiting, and having nothing to do but wait.

The people who couldn't be completely healed were sent on the transports to Paraguay. So when I realized that it was taking so long to get approval for me to go to North America, I finally told Peter and Siegfried that it didn't matter where I went. I just didn't want to stay in Germany. Germany felt so close to Poland to me, I was still afraid that someone would come and send me back to those camps. If I hadn't had uncles in America and Canada, I may not have had the idea to leave Europe, but now I knew that I couldn't stay. I wanted to go someplace far away.

When I was finally ready to go, they sent me on another train to an emigration office at Fallingbostel. There I had to have another medical exam. There were lots of other people there being examined too. We had to wait a long time, and people would come out of the exam and start to cry because they had not passed. It was so sad. But I came through with no problem whatsoever. Everything was okay.

Many other MCC people also went with me to Fallingbostel. Then we came back to Gronau, and they said that since my medical exam was okay, I was almost ready to emigrate. All that remained was to go to the Consulate to get my passport. So they sent us to Lemgo on a train.

I was so nervous! We refugees all filed into a big room where there was a long table against one wall. Behind the table were three men from the consulates. One was from the American Consulate, one was from the Canadian Consulate, and one was from the Polish Consulate! I thought, "Oh! Why do I have to go to the Polish

Consulate?" I was so scared when I found out where he was from! I thought that if he found out that I had come over the border illegally, he would send me back.

My heart was pounding so hard! I came to the first man, who looked at my stack of papers and put his stamp on it. The second man looked at me and asked me some questions about where I was born. He also asked if the information on the papers was correct. I said, "Yes," and he pounded his stamp on them. Then I came to the last one, the Polish one.

He had a little notebook on the table in front of him. He opened that book and turned it around so it was facing me. Then in Polish, he said, "Read it." It said, "Ufstan'na prawej nodze." I will never forget that in my life. "Stand on your right foot," it said. Since I was so nervous, and scared about what they would do with me, I read it and I actually lifted my left foot!

The men laughed a little bit, and the Polish official turned the book around. Then he picked up my papers, stamped them, and I was ready to go!

I never understood what that was about. When I got back to Gronau, I told Peter Dyck what had happened, he just shook his head and said, "Das ist aber spassig!" And he laughed, he thought that was strange. He had never heard from other refugees that such a thing happened.

After that it did not take long before I was ready to leave. Finally they put us on another train and sent us to Bremen, where our ship was waiting. By this time I had a suitcase full of clothes to take with me. I had the clothes that Rachel had given me, and the clothes I had gotten at Gronau. During my year in Germany, my uncles in North America wrote to me and asked what I needed. So they sent me packages of coffee and tea. I didn't use the coffee and tea myself, but sold it in the stores in Gronau to get a little money. Then I could use the money to buy some things that I needed, like a suitcase. I thought that if I was going to travel, I should have a suitcase. So with that money from the coffee and tea, I bought myself a little suitcase.

Elfrieda had given me a pair of shoes at Gronau, but since my feet were so big, I had to wear men's shoes. I didn't care, as long as I had some shoes. But I thought that when I went to Canada, I should have some good shoes.

My cousin in Philadelphia, who was two years older than me, wrote me letters too, asking me what I needed. And I wrote back to her, but I didn't have money for an envelope or a stamp. So Lois Yake gave me an envelope, and paper to write on. And when I was finished, I gave the letter to Lois, and she even paid for the stamp and sent it for me! That's the way they treated us at Gronau. We never had money, but we always had what we needed.

My cousin wrote to me and asked if I needed bedding or towels. I wrote back and said that we had bedding, but if she would send a couple towels I would be very grateful. So she did. And I still have one of those towels! It was my towel that I used to dry myself at Gronau. And I've kept it. It was so special to me that I wanted to keep it as long as I could, my towel from Philadelphia. But it has gotten so old that I can't use it to dry myself anymore. So now when I bake bread I use it to put under the pans with the dough. Four loaves will fit on top of this towel. I wrote to my cousin a few years ago and told her that I still had her towel, and told her what I use it for now.

When she wrote to me in Gronau, she also asked if I needed clothes. I am the type of person that when I have the necessary things, I am happy. I don't need anything else. But I did need some stockings and some shoes. She wrote me back and asked me what size I needed. I hadn't even thought of that! Shoes are shoes, I thought. But we could have had very different sizes of feet. So I wrote back and told her what size I wore.

Then she wrote back and said, "We don't measure the European way." So she told me to take a piece of writing paper and trace the outline of my foot on the paper. On one side of the paper I traced my foot, and on the other side I wrote the letter. And she sent me a good pair of shoes, black shoes for Sunday. I had them for nearly ten years, they fit so nicely.

In Pelplin, Rachel had given me a nice blanket. It was a dark green wool army-style blanket. I thought it would make such a nice coat. But when I left to walk through the Russian Zone of Germany, I could not take it with me, and since it was summertime, I didn't need it for warmth. So Menno brought it to Gronau with the rest of my things.

When I was in Gronau, there was a place where they dyed cloth. I didn't like the green of the blanket, it was so much like the army. So I took that blanket to this place and asked them to dye it navy blue in exchange for a pound of coffee. But I didn't sew that blanket into a coat myself. Gronau was a small town, and after awhile we knew many people who lived in the town. I knew a seamstress in town who could sew my coat for me, so I took it to her. I gave her a pound of coffee or tea too, as payment.

So now I had a nice coat, a good pair of shoes, and a suitcase. I felt like a real traveler! When I came from Poland, I didn't want to carry a suitcase because looking like a traveler then would have been a bad thing. With just my small bag, I could have just been going into town for the day. People would be less suspicious, I thought. But now I had a real suitcase and good clothes to wear.

We traveled by train to Bremen and got on the big boat, the Samaria. And I thought to myself: my adventures in Europe as a refugee are finally at an end. Canada, here I come!

But as it turned out, Europe wasn't yet quite finished with me! Indeed, I was still in for an astounding surprise.

Before I left Poland, I had given Menno the names of my sister, my mother, and my father, to include on his list of missing persons. So many people were separated from their families, and there were groups like the Red Cross and MCC who were working to locate lost family members. It often took a long time to find people, but many people were reunited with loved ones eventually. I put these same names on another list when I reached Gronau, hoping that someone would turn up. Menno had already found my Aunt Wanda in that big camp in Poland. Later on she was able to come out of Poland, too. I was already in Canada when she came. But that was the only person in my family that he found while I was at Gronau.

When we were sent to Bremen, we had to wait there for ten days. I remember we were all still pretty scared. We weren't on the water yet, they could still send us back. I thought that once we were on the water nobody could catch us anymore! But we still had to wait there for ten days.

We could see our boat at the dock, and there were 10,000 people waiting to get on other boats. There were 35 of us from Gronau who were waiting, and the others were Jews and Ukrainians and refugees from all over, waiting for their ships. Bremen was a big port city, where they processed all the refugees leaving Germany. There was a large group of people who were waiting to go to Brazil. And some were waiting to go to the United States, and others were going to Canada.

We all wanted to know why we had to wait for ten days. The officials told us that they had to get everything loaded on the ship, but later we heard that they were also waiting for 300 French people to arrive.

Two or three days after I got there, a telegram came for me from Gronau. It said that I should come back to the camp, they had found my Mother! I didn't have any money at all, but MCC sent me a ticket so that I could return to see my Mom. "How long can I stay?" I asked. They told me that I had four days. I could come back to Gronau and at least see Mom and talk with her a bit, but then they would send me back to Bremen so I could get on the ship.

They told me to just go to the train station, my ticket had been paid for and everything was ready. So I went back to Gronau. My Mom was there when I got off the train! When I think back, I can hardly believe that it was true. But she really was there. We hadn't seen each other for three years – but very long years they were, from 1945 to 1948. It had seemed like forever!

Mom told me that after I had been chased out of my home into prison camp, she had remained at home for another week. My sister Emma, with her two small children, had also come home. Polish guards locked them in the basement. Some Poles who knew us – including Sophia, our hired girl – would come at night and throw some bread in to them through an open window.

During this time some guards demanded money and gold, and when Mom said she had none, one guard threatened to take Mom out, put her against the wall, and shoot her. But then another guard came along and said, "No, no, she is a good German woman." After about a week, all four were taken to prison camp. Mom was more fortunate than some other older women who couldn't work as well. Sometimes guards would just kick around these women until they would fall, dead – or they pushed them into the water.

Mom was able to work. She had food to eat, and some clothes – not much – but she had things to wear. For a long time she lived close to Warsaw, working for a farmer. One day the police came and told her they were taking her to the station. She was scared, wondering where they would send her now. They put her on a train and sent her out of Poland, through Berlin, and on to Gronau where she arrived just before I was ready to cross the ocean. She didn't know what was happening, or who had arranged for her to leave. They just put her on that train. Later, she thought that maybe it was the Red Cross, or MCC.

We talked and cried together so much, but then the headache started. I had waited a year for my papers to come through, and finally they were ready. I had gone through so much to get everything in order. We were so happy to be together, and I thought that now I should stay with her. She was older already, and I could take care of her. And I know it was so hard for her too. I was so close to getting on the boat, and I had to leave already. She wanted to have me with her too.

We talked to Peter Dyck and asked if there was some way they could take my papers back and maybe send somebody else in my place. I wanted to stay with Mother, and help work on her papers so she could come with me. "No, no, Fräulein Schroeder," he said. "Go quickly, we'll have to start with your mother from the very beginning."

They had to give her a medical examination, and take her to the Consulate and do everything to get her papers in order. And then Peter told me that I had barely made it through. He said that the Polish Consulate was ready to throw my papers in the wastebasket and send me back to Poland.

Well, when I heard that, I got scared and thought too that I had better go on and go to Canada, or else I would never be able to leave. So I talked to Mother about it. And she said I should go ahead. Peter Dyck told us that if I was there already, she would have a good chance of coming to join me. And I knew they would take very good care of her at Gronau. They told me they would feed her and give her a place to stay while she waited to come.

Siegfried Janzen agreed with Peter that it would be best for me to proceed with my plans and go. So that's what we decided to do. Mom came with me to the station, along with some other friends, and she said good-bye to me there at the train. I went back to Bremen and got on that boat to come to Canada.

We left the Bremen port in the afternoon. The trip took us eleven days, but it seemed very long. When we were all boarded, there was an orchestra which played for us. They played marches and military songs like I had heard during the war. But they played them to say farewell to those of us on the boat. And we were saying farewell to Europe. I knew that the Lord would be with me, and that I was going to see my uncle in Canada. Those two thoughts gave me my feet to stand on in that boat.

There were lots of people on the shore who had come to wave good-bye to us. When we were close to the dock, the water was calm, but a little farther out, the waves started getting really big. As long as we could see land, we were all right, people could stand firmly on the boat's deck. But when we got out of sight of the land, the boat started to rock more, and people started to get sick. Lots of people were throwing up. It was maybe only an hour or two into the trip, and already people were so seasick! They would just lie there, they couldn't move or anything. And the men who worked on the boat, and who were used to the rocking, would come with their big mops and clean the floor.

They put the girls and single women in one room together. The ship was four stories deep into the water and four stories above – it was a very big ship. There were sixty of us women, all kept in the same room. We were below deck. I guess the single men had their own section, and families had another section.

When we were at sea, the boat really started to rock. I was sleeping on a top bunk, and I thought the high waves would throw me out of bed! And my stomach hurt so badly. I'll never forget one Polish woman's anguish. She wailed, "My stomach is going to pieces; I came through the war alive, but now I will die of seasickness here on this boat!" But a nurse came around and talked to us. She said, "Try to keep from throwing up. If you can just try to swallow and keep it down, you will get used to it." And she was right. I was so close to vomiting, I could feel it at the top of my throat. But once I learned to keep it down, I could get by.

Everything hurt, though. My stomach hurt and everything hurt, but I managed to keep my food down. We stayed below deck when the weather was bad. One sunny day when the water was fairly calm, we were allowed to come outside to the deck. I remember climbing up to the deck and looking at the sky.

Sometimes we could go outside when the waves were high but not too dangerous. Then the water was such a deep, deep blue! It was as if the boat traveled down into a huge ravine, and then it climbed right up the other side. The waves tossed us this way and then that way, it was so rough.

In the hallway where we walked to get our food, they had posted a map of the ocean. And each day they put pins on the map to show where we were, and how much farther we still had to sail to get to Halifax, Nova Scotia. When we were halfway there, we were so thankful!

They fed us good food on the ship. There was a long dining room with long tables. They served us ham (we never saw that during the war, or at Gronau!) and mashed potatoes and fruit, and desserts – Jell-O with fruit in it. It was like being at a wedding every day! The men took care of us, they would bring coffee and tea too.

The tables were so full and beautiful, yet nobody could eat. Everyone was so sick from the motion of the ship. One day a woman who was sitting beside me, leaned over and said, "Oh, how I would love some sauerkraut now!"

"Sauerkraut!" said the waiter. And he disappeared into the kitchen. It did not take long before he returned with a big dish full of sauerkraut. Everybody was looking at that dish so hungrily. I was too, it looked so good. And, you know, it seemed that after we had that sauerkraut, we got our appetites back a little bit. We could eat better then.

In addition to the good meals they cooked for us, they also gave us apples and oranges outside our sleeping quarters. I thought, "Oh, my, how nice this is, it couldn't be any better!" Many people had brought along books to read. I didn't have a book, but I wished so badly that I did. The days were so long when I didn't have anything to do except look at the water and wait for mealtimes. So later, when other people were finished with their books, I asked them if I could borrow their books to read. But in the beginning I just knitted most of the time. I had some old wool sweaters and I ripped apart the yarn, tied it together, and made myself a new vest. I had that vest for many years.

They had entertainment too. I remember a room where they

had games and things for people to do. But all those English games were hard for me, checkers and chess and so forth. So I didn't spend too much time there. I mostly sat and visited with people.

The day before we arrived in Halifax, they took us into a room where there were some offices, and they gave us each five dollars for spending money. There was a little canteen or store on the ship where we could spend our money. The store had chocolates and candy, and chewing gum. We didn't even know what chewing gum was then! And they had toothbrushes and writing papers. So I thought I would buy myself a new toothbrush. My old one was in pretty bad shape – it was the one Rachel had given me. And I bought some toothpaste and writing paper, and after all that, I still had some money left. So I bought myself some chocolate.

I ate that chocolate, even though my stomach was still kind of upset from being on the boat. And after that, I thought, "What did I do?!" I didn't feel very well. And since then I haven't liked chocolates anymore.

When we got to Halifax, I was so happy to see land again. They unloaded us immediately from the boat and put us on the train that was waiting for us there. MCC workers were waiting for us too, to help us onto the train. I didn't get to see anything of Halifax, so I don't really remember what it looked like.

The train left right away, and we rode through the night. We rode the train to Kitchener, Ontario. There were all kinds of people on the boat, and when we got off, people scattered here and there. Some people stayed in Halifax, others got off the train in Montreal. Many people from our group of Mennonites got off the train in Kitchener. A handful came all the way to Winnipeg – maybe six or so. And only Walli Ossenkopf, her son Hans, her mother and I continued beyond Winnipeg.

I remember seeing many lakes on our way across. There were lots of little lakes and many trees, and tiny villages scattered here and there – and the endless prairies. At one point we said, "Oh, there is no end to Canada!" And I thought, "Where are we going? Germany was so nice."

There were MCC people in Winnipeg too. There was a kitchen on the train from Kitchener to Winnipeg, and so they served us food. But I can't remember what we ate. When we got to Winnipeg, the train stopped for a couple hours. There, MCC workers gave us each five dollars to buy some food. So I went to a store nearby and bought some bread and some tomatoes.

We had another seven or eight hours to go yet, and this time we wouldn't have any food on the train. It was in August when we came across, and the dust was flying! I had on a blue dress with a white collar, and the collar got so dirty and black inside. There was no water on the train that we could use for washing. We could not flush the toilets, and we couldn't wash our hands. But I thought, "Who cares? I am finally near the end of my journey!"

Notes:

[1] On December 7, 1948, Edna handed in to the MCC Gronau administration a hand-written Lebenslauf, *or vita, which MCC retained in its archives (see the original German document, with translation, below in the Documents section).*

[2] On November 4, 1949, Siegfried Janzen (Director of the MCC-Gronau office), issued a general report, reaching back to the time Edna was there (an excerpt of which is published below in the Documents section).

[3] A few months before Edna arrived in Gronau, someone described with a poetic touch "One Day in an MCC Camp" (a translation of which is published below in the Documents section).

NEW LIFE UNDER A VAST SKY

When people asked me where in Canada I was going, I told them, "to Drah-keh, Saskatchewan" I pronounced Drake in the Polish way – "Drah-keh." I knew I was supposed to get off the train in Lanigan. The conductor told me that, and he said he would let me know when we arrived. Then I was supposed to take a smaller train to Drake, where my Uncle Edmund and Aunt Lydia lived.

I got off the train in Lanigan, and standing there was a man who looked just like my father! "Sind Sie es?" ("Is it you?"), I asked. "You must be my uncle!" And he said, "Yes, I'm your Uncle Edmund." Then I gave him a big hug. He and Aunt Lydia had driven from Drake to pick me up, so I didn't have to get on the second train.

It was so dusty there! A gust of wind would come by and send the dust flying. My Aunt Lydia was sitting in the car – a big, black, rounded car. She was watching to see what would happen. I was the only person who got off the train.

Usually the arrangement was that if someone paid for your trip over to America, you would stay with them for a year and work to pay off your fare. Then after a year you would be free to go where you liked. So since my Uncle Edmund had paid for me to come to Canada, I went to stay with him.

I had heard already that Saskatchewan was very cold. Menno Fast had told me that in Poland. And people at Gronau told me that British Columbia was much warmer, and that in B.C. there were many fruit trees, so it would feel like home. I thought that I would work for my uncle for a year, and then if I didn't find a job I liked, I would move to B.C.

But my plans changed. Around Christmas time, Henry Thiessen, the son of Russian Mennonite immigrants, started to come for visits. His family went to the same church as my aunt and uncle.

My aunt and uncle were like my second family, and soon Uncle Edmund started pointing out that there was a young man who was interested in me.

But I said to Uncle, "I did not come to Canada to get married." I felt like I was fifty years old, and those in between years were all gone. I said, "No I'm just not ready to have a boyfriend." But every now and then Henry still came around.

One of the reasons it seemed like a good idea for us to date was that my cousin was going with Henry's sister. Since traveling was difficult in those days, they thought that whenever Eugene and Annie would visit each other, Henry and I could visit too – all four of us could date together. We could go to church together, have dinner at the Thiessen's house and then come back together.

But still I said to aunt and uncle, "I love you so much, but I just have to say no." I felt like I needed time to heal from everything, to get adjusted and learn the language. It just felt too early. I'd had other chances to have a boyfriend in Europe. In Gronau, there was one boy who thought he just *had* to date me! I was friendly to everybody, and when it came to friendship, I was fine. But I was not interested in anything serious. I thought I would never marry! In our village back home, marriages were always between people who had known each other their whole lives. And all the boys I had known were dead. So I thought I would never get married. I thought I could never marry someone I hadn t known from when I was a child. So I talked about this with Auntie and Uncle and they said, "Okay, we won't push you."

When the winter came, there was not much to do. I was so thankful I could sew and crochet. My uncle had two daughters at home, and there was another cousin there who could sew too. Uncle Peter and Aunt Florence came to Canada a month after I did, and they stayed with Uncle Edmund too. So the house was full. There were so many women in that house, we would sew a dress in a day! Would anyone like a dress for Easter? Would anyone like a dress for the summer? It was no problem. On Saturdays I helped clean the house, but that's nearly all we did – sewing and cleaning.

The women in that household were so organized: some cooked, some washed the dishes. Order was necessary since there were so many people in the same house. We were family, together. They all showed me so much love. I had truly become part of their family.[1]

When I was baptized at the refugee camp in Gronau, I wanted to be part of the Mennonite Brethren Church, like my Grandma. So I was glad when I came to Saskatchewan that my aunt and uncle went to a Mennonite Brethren Church. When Uncle Peter came, though, he went to the church in Drake. They don't have communion as often there as we do at Philadelphia Church. Here we have it the first Sunday of every month.

In the beginning when I came here, I thought people would point at me and think, She is a poor refugee. Even at church I felt that everyone else was from Canada, I was the only "foreigner". This made me different, I felt. It took a while until that feeling disappeared and I could mix in with others. Now I feel we are all family – church family. I appreciate this family so much!

Mennonite church life in Poland before the war was a little different from the way we do things here. There we did not have Sunday school, did not have prayer meetings as we do here during the week, or church meetings in the evenings. The people worked all week: "Six days you are to work, and on the seventh day, you are to rest." Sunday – the rest day – we went to church and worshipped together and visited in the afternoon. But I soon got used to the differences and now I appreciate the way church life is here.

Language made church a bit difficult for me. At first we spoke German like we had in Poland, and I could understand everything. But eventually we switched to English, and I couldn't understand anything. Finally I learned enough English to follow, and now it really feels like home.

During my first year in Canada, in the evenings I would sit and talk with my aunt and uncle. They told me stories about my Dad and asked me questions about what had happened to him. They wanted to know what life was like in Poland during the war, what the Germans did to us, and what the Poles did to us. And I responded, at least for a while. We would sit and cry, late at night. They kept it to themselves, but they just wanted to know. They had heard some things in the news about what it was like in Europe, and wondered, for example, whether the horrible stories told about the Jews were true.

Uncle Edmund was very close to my Dad, they were born only

a year apart. Before the war, the younger men had to go into the Polish military for three years' training. Dad and Uncle Edmund were in training together. Usually the military separated brothers, but they were lucky to be together.

After the war everything in the house, including all our pictures, was ransacked and destroyed. But Uncle Edmund had a picture of himself and my Dad, taken in their uniforms. He showed it to me and he said, "As long as I am alive, I would like to keep it, but when I am no longer here, it will be yours." He even told this to his daughter. He told her to give that picture to me, so I would have something from my Dad. Then they also gave me another picture. My cousin said, "I will give you this picture, too." It is a picture taken at my grandfather s funeral, and my Dad and Mom are on it as well.

So now I have two pictures of my Dad, and they are very important to me. In them Uncle Edmund and Dad look very much like twins. My Dad would tell me things about his life, but I was only a little girl at the time, and it would go in one ear and out the other. Then, it had not been so important to me to hear the stories. But when I came to Canada, and my uncle told me things about that time, it was different. My Father and my uncle grew up together, went to school together, worked together. From my Uncle Edmund I found out quite a bit about how my Dad grew up.

Although my Uncle asked me many questions, I did not tell him my whole story. I simply talked about this or that, whatever he would ask. For a while, I would answer his questions, but I had to stop because I would dream such terrible nightmares. I could no longer continue talking about Europe. But by then, they had heard a lot of the details, how my Dad was taken away and what happened after he was gone. We still don t know – perhaps we ll never know – how his life ended.

In my nightmares the Russians would shoot, and the Poles would shoot, and I would run and run and run, endlessly. I would fall into deep, deep water, and then I would wake up. In other dreams I had returned to Poland, and someone would steal my purse and my passport. Then I wondered how I would get back to Canada. Sometimes I dreamed I was opening a door, trying to get out somewhere, and screaming all the while.

I had nightmares even after Henry and I were married. But I

didn't even need to talk about these things to experience nightmares. Just thinking about Poland brought them on, and at night I would dream horrible dreams about bombing and burning, and sometimes I would wake up with the moon shining in the window, and I would be afraid that our house was burning – things like that. I knew I would have to try to forget, and not think about these things. Eventually it did get better.

Close to Easter, I started to reconsider about Henry. I guess the winter was long and I had plenty of time to think about it and pray about it. He was such a nice young man, and he had the kind of character, the qualities I would have looked for in a husband.

So finally I said yes, I would marry him. I surprised myself by saying yes so soon! But I have never regretted it. I couldn't wish for a better husband. I talk much more than he does, he's kind of quiet. But I usually know what he thinks and what he wants, and it has worked out so well. The Lord has been good to me.

We were married on the first of June, 1950. We had a double wedding with Eugene and Annie, Henry's sister. The day after the wedding, the four of us drove to Saskatoon to have our wedding pictures taken. When we were finished with that, Eugene and Henry thought we needed a little something special, so they bought us ice cream. That was such a treat!

After the wedding Henry and I moved onto a farm across the road from his parents, close to Watrous. We started with a few dairy cows, some chickens and some pigs. We sold the eggs and the cream – at that time the milk went for the pigs. We had two quarters of land that we farmed with wheat and barley, and we had a garden for our vegetables. So the farm provided our income. The house was small, but it was our house and I was so thankful to have it! We heated the house with a wood stove, and when it was so bitter cold, we added coal to the wood.

In those first years, the winters were so cold and long. That was the hardest thing for me to get used to! We usually had ice on the windows an inch thick! And it seemed that the cold came in through the walls. At night it was so cold that sometimes in the morning when I was making the beds, the pillows were stuck – frozen fast to the bed! So I waited a while until it warmed up, and they eventually came unstuck.

Sometimes I liked to look out to see what Henry was doing in the yard. I would make a little hole in the ice on the window and watch him walking around, and it felt good. I liked that the windows were all covered up. I thought no one would see me from outside – no policemen, no soldiers. That feeling continued for a long time.

My Mom was still in Gronau for three years after I came to Canada. I think she could have come sooner, but she wanted to find Emma, my sister. She believed that Emma was still alive, and she felt that Canada was too far away. She wanted to know for certain that Emma was alive.

The MCC workers were still looking for Emma and her two boys. One of the boys died, but they found Emma's youngest boy, Edmund. They arranged for him to get out of Poland, and he came to Gronau. He even started to go to school there. Since Mom was with him, she said she couldn't come to Canada yet. Then through Menno Fast, I believe, they found Emma in a camp in Poland. But she couldn't come out right away. She had married a second time, and her new husband was a Polish man. I think that if she had been single she could have come right away, but as it was they didn't let her.

The Iron Curtain was in place then, and the government wasn't letting any Polish people out. After a few years, MCC closed down its unit in Gronau. Most of the emigration had finished, so their job was finished, and they were closing everything down. Peter Dyck wrote to us from Germany and said that if we would send $350 each month, they would rent Mom an apartment there so she could wait for Emma to come out of Poland. At that time we were so poor, we could not afford $350 each month.

So we prayed about it and talked with Mom and Dad Thiessen, and we decided to gather up the money so Mom and Emma's son, Edmund, could come and live with us here. We somehow scraped the money together, and paid for their trip. And we moved a little house onto our yard for Mom to live in. The house was in Drake, and we bought it and moved it with a trailer to our yard.

Mom and Edmund came in the Spring of 1953. We were so happy to have her here. And she was pretty content here, I think. But she always had one wish, that she could see Emma again, and that Emma would be reunited with Edmund, her son. It took ten years from when Emma was first found in Poland, but it finally happened. We worked with her papers, and wrote back and forth. We sent letters to Ottawa, and to the immigration offices. But the Polish government would not let her out.

In those years there was an MCC office in Winnipeg. When we worked with my sister's papers, we wrote to the immigration office there. Later, MCC set up an office in Saskatoon. They told us then that we should go to the office in Saskatoon and talk with the people there about my sister. So we did.

There was an MCC man there who asked us to tell him our story, and why we wanted Emma to come. We told him that her son, Edmund, was here, as well as our mother, and we wanted to reunite the family. The man listened to us as we talked, then he filled out some papers, and said that he would do everything he could to help her. In three months, Emma was here in Canada, along with her second husband! I think that MCC man in Saskatoon must have really known the best way to make it happen.

Edmund was nearly grown by the time his mother was finally allowed to emigrate. He was living with us, and he was just like another son to us. We sent him to the public school here.

Edmund was ready for high school when Emma finally came. I remember taking him to the train station here in Watrous to see his Mom for the first time since before he could remember. Henry and I had three sons then – Harvey, Bernie and John – and we brought them with us to the station. Edmund was sixteen by then, and he looked so big. He was a tall, slim fellow.

The train pulled up, and Emma and her husband Frank got off. I recognized her. She looked the same, only much rounder than before. We hugged and cried for a while. And then I said, "Emma, this is your son Edmund." She turned and looked at him, but it seemed like she didn't really see him. Then her eyes focused on our son John. She went and picked up John, who was only five, and held this little boy – Edmund had been so small when they took him away from her.

Then I was crying, and I put my hand on her shoulder and said, "No Emma, not the little boy; over here is your son!" and I pointed to Edmund. Emma looked up, and then I could see in her eyes that she understood. And she held Edmund so tightly, she didn't want to let him go.

Emma came in May and stayed with us just a few days. We said they could stay with us longer, and we would feed them. But we could not pay them wages, so they wouldn't have any money of their own. We did the best we could, but that's when they decided to move to Regina, which is about 130 kilometers from where we were living. Uncle Edmund had found her a job and a place to live there, so she moved there. Edmund, Emma s son, had to stay with us until he finished his school at the end of June. And then he stayed a little longer, since he was so used to us by then. But soon Emma wrote and said that now he should come live with her in Regina.

While they were still with us, we all ate together, and Mom cooked good sauerkraut and we visited. Mom was finally with Emma. We had planned for Mom to stay with us on the farm during the summer months, when the weather was nice. And in the winter she wanted to go live with Emma in Regina, since they had better heating and water. It was all nicely planned.

But soon after Emma left for Regina, Mom became very sick. The doctor said she had cancer of the liver, but she actually died of a blood clot one night. The doctor didn't expect her to die so suddenly. It was so quick that Emma didn't even have a chance to come and be with her while she was dying. That was very hard for Emma, and for me too. But with the years we kind of heal and let those things rest.

We never found out what happened to my Dad. Two or three civilians, along with a Polish soldier, took him from us. We were so scared, so very scared. We were just crying and crying. If they had only been civilians, then Dad might have said that he had some rights as a *Dorfschulze*. But since they brought the soldier along, and it was wartime, he simply had to go.

Later on, some soldiers told my sister they had taken Dad to a forest, maybe a kilometer and a half or two away, where under some trees they shot him. One soldier said, "Don't cry about your Dad, he's already dead."

Still later on, while I was yet in Germany, I wrote to a Polish girl to find out if she had learned anything about what had happened to my Dad. She had heard that the men who had been taken that day, along with Dad, were put on a train and sent to Siberia. So we still don't know what the truth is.

In any case, I never heard more. And that's pretty hard for me. It would be hard if I knew that they had shot him, and where his grave was. But that would have been easier than not knowing. Even now I live in hope. Now that I am older I think my Dad and I will meet pretty soon in heaven.

Notes:

[1] Around this time (December 14, 1949), Edna wrote a letter to MCC Gronau Director Siegfried (and Margaret) Janzen (published in translation, below, in the Documents section).

THE WALL

Epilogue

I have never, up to now, been able to tell my whole story. I had shared only a few glimpses of my war years with my relatives during my first months in Canada, but soon stopped reflecting on these things for the sake of my own emotional health. Over the years I have also told a little bit here and there to my husband – about life in the prison camps, and how hard it was when they took my Dad away. And he felt sorry for all these things that had happened that were now past, things that had been done to me in wartime that will remain with me probably as long as I shall live. At the same time, I was glad that he did not ask too much.

And I was glad that nobody else asked me about my story! Nobody here in the church asked anything. Even among our friends here, not one question about what had happened to me before I came to Canada.

During the wartime I did not have good friends. My close friends from school and church all died or were taken away during the war. During my early years here in Saskatchewan, I located some old acquaintances from Poland. Some of them lived in British Columbia, some lived in Winnipeg. But most were elderly, and soon died. So when I came here, I thought I was the only person from my home area to escape alive. I felt that way for years.

One person stands out during all this time – Rachel Fisher. In 1948, after all the horrible things stopped, and that chapter of the war years and the years of prison camp ended, there was Rachel. That first day when I saw Rachel, she looked like an angel standing before me. I once again discovered friendship. For some reason, I trusted her immediately.

Otherwise, in the war and in the prison camps we did not trust people, we did not make friends, and we did not care. I was no longer used to making friends. But when I met the Fishers, a new chapter in my life began.

During those years I was especially suspicious of men. These were the years of the black market, when spies were everywhere. What if Bob, when he met me in Warsaw had been a spy? Later on I thought, "Oh, what did I do!" I had told Bob about my intentions to escape. He could easily have been a spy trying to find out my plans so he could report me to the Polish government. I don't know why I trusted. How could I trust, after experiencing all those frightening and dark years? Yet somehow a voice was telling me to trust, and I did.

I can tell you, war is hard, and it happens so quickly! German cannons could strike with pinpoint accuracy from 20 and more miles away, aiming to kill and destroy as much as they could. And they had horrible flame throwers that set everything ablaze. Russian tanks would just roll over people. Planes from both sides flew overhead and bombed, and then they would circle back to shoot everything they could with machine guns. After the war, the new Polish government could not find the many German government officials who had already fled, to kill them or to take them prisoner. So instead, they took prisoner those "enemies" who remained -- mothers and children, women of all ages, and some older men who had survived the whole thing. Surviving the horrendous and shameful things that happened after the war was the hardest part.

I thought, What did we do to deserve being locked in these dreadful prison camps? To myself I said, simply, it's wartime. This is the only way that I could understand it. The children and old people have to suffer too. Fighting in war is very hard. The cannons spit their fire, and the tanks roll over people and there is so much death. But after that, when the front moves on, the civilians have to suffer so much too.

First of all, there s no food, and you re separated from your family and taken from your home. It was so hard for me to hear the babies crying, their daddies were gone and their mothers could do little to help them. This was harder for me than the bombs and shooting. Day after day I had to look at all this misery as a person, still existing, who did not want to exist.

During all these experiences I tried hard to be calm and forgiving. Even while they were beating me up I said to myself, "Oh, if I could just help you men and show you what you are doing!" I even felt sorry for them, they had allowed themselves to stoop to such depths. I think the Lord gave this attitude and spirit to me as part of my nature. I think I am very much like my Dad – I learned so much from him.

Throughout this whole time, I was so thankful I was as young as I was. I had my health; in fact, I don't remember ever being sick throughout all those war and prison years. I did not know what a cough was, or a headache, or a cold! Numerous times typhoid would break out and many others would just collapse. Many a morning we would wake up and tramp to the door over the people who were dead and dying. Yet somehow I did not experience sickness. However, I was afflicted with a different type of disease: terror. So great was my terror that often I shook all over.

While walking through East Germany, I was thankful I was alone, thankful I was not married. I had no husband to cry about. I had no children, no baby to cry about. So even in that loneliness, I knew I did not have to cry. I was doing this by myself.

Of course, I missed my family. I did not know where anyone was. But when I saw in the filthy camps other mothers with babies, so hungry and so cold, just skin and bones and barely able to walk, I thought that things were easier for me. I was alone. And I often thanked God that I was alone.

When I arrived on this side of the ocean, I built up a wall, closing off what I had left behind. I entered into a new life on this side of the wall. I did not want to talk about what had happened before. I was not at all sure that people here would understand. And since in most cases nobody asked me about my past, I thought, why should I talk about it?

During the following 40 years I kept quiet about my life in Europe. Rachel Fisher was the first person who heard the whole story, just a few years ago. Rachel said, "Edna, we have known you since that day when you arrived at MCC in 1948. But what was your story before then, what was your experience during the war?" And so Rachel and I sat and talked, just the two of us. Then I was ready to tell my whole story. I thought carefully about my memories kept behind the high wall I had built, and said, yes, I can talk about them now. I want to talk about them now.

I think I was ready because it was Rachel who had asked – a dear friend – but also because she had been a central part of my experience. My heart was ready by this time to share with someone

I could trust. It has occurred to me that maybe my nightmares would come back, but they never bother me any more. I am okay.

During those forty years my wall protected me. My dreaming stopped. I thought of those years from 1939 to 1948 as a chapter of my existence which I needed to leave behind. I had to begin a new chapter.

I think the wall has now come down – at least in part. I guess it will not disappear completely. I have not talked with other people who survived the war years about how to handle the memories. I think the war will stay with those of us who lived through it. But for me, now, the memories are easier to handle. And yet, around here, I have nobody to talk to about it, no one who went through the same experiences. So even today I don't talk about it very often. But I think it has helped me to share the story with Rachel and others. And I am glad it is now down in black and white for my grandchildren, and for others who might want to know my story.

As I look back on all my wartime experiences, I do not wish to blame one group or another for what happened. It was war, and perhaps no one could prevent what happened. The best thing would have been for the Germans simply to have left us alone, and allowed us to live in Poland as we had always lived. We had our villages and our families and we lived in peace. Before the war, the Polish people never called us Germans, or "Hitler stooges." Although I suffered all those years – starving, freezing, and alone – from my heart, I forgive them all. It was war. The only thing that allows me to continue living is forgiveness.

In German, there is a word, *loslassen* – literally, letting-go. I could be angry at the Germans for what they did, I could be angry at the Poles for what they did, but I don't want to live in anger. That's what I mean by loslassen – letting go both within and without, and freeing myself of the chaos that had so long entangled me.

Sometimes I think about all the hard things we've lived through, and I wonder how we did it. Those early years here in Saskatchewan were sometimes hard too. We worked hard, but we had the courage and strength to do what we had to do. And we were content. We were thankful for everything the Lord gave us. And the times kept getting better. The Lord blessed us with five sons, five daughters-in-law and nine grandchildren. I am thankful for so many things.

I do not think I am stronger than other people, or that I am somehow more special. I could not have survived without God, who helped me through. Somehow, at the time, God in his graciousness numbed the minds of those of us who experienced such horrible things. How else could we have survived such physical torture and emotional terror and humiliation? And I hope that in telling my story it will help others to see how good God is, and how faith can help us survive even in the hardest of times. The Lord was with me in my long walk toward the light and I have come to know peace.

III

EDNA'S STORY,
PICTORIALLY

On that fateful day in 1945 when she was forcibly taken from her home, never to see it again, Edna was from one moment to the next separated not only from family, but also from all her possessions, including photographs.

Edna was never again to see her home, which had been ransacked, everything of monetary value taken, and her precious photographs, books, and correspondence destroyed. Only much later could Edna begin to build a new, albeit slim, collection of visual memories, one photograph at a time, from relatives who, too, had emigrated to Canada.

What follows are pre-1945 photographs which came together in this one-by-one fashion, over a period of years, indeed, decades. MCC personnel Bob and Rachel Fisher, and Menno Fast, among others, supplied many of the photographs taken in 1948 and 49. The third grouping of photographs are of Edna, with family and friends, taken since the year of her arrival in Saskatchewan, in 1949.

Edna, as a schoolgirl, ca. 1940 or 41 [left]; and [right] as a smiling teenager just having turned thirteen (July 22, 1939), before the War began.

Edna's Father, David Schroeder [left], and her Uncle, Edmund Schroeder [right], in Polish military uniforms (1922). David was 22 and Edmund, 21. All young men at that time were required to serve in the military for three years, whether or not there was a war. David was not yet married to Edna's mother, Augusta (they were married ca. 1924).

[Top:] *Edna (at 18) [left] and Leah, her cousin and best friend, in Czerwinsk, where Edna was working at the mill. Leah had come by bike to visit, and they had their picture taken by a photographer in town.*

[Bottom, from right to left:] *Edna, her brother Robert, Robert's wife Olga, and Edna's brother Edmund, at German-occupied Königsberg in East Prussia, ca. 1940 or 41. The photo was taken about two weeks before the family received word of Edmund's death on the front.*

[Top:] The Deutsch Kazun Mennonite Church, built in 1892, where Edna and her parents attended, at which time the building had also served as a school. In the 1990s the building was a private residence.
[Bottom:] The Deutsch Wysmysle Mennonite Church (Mennonite Brethren), built in 1864, was a Mennonite meetinghouse until 1945. In the 1990s it was used for seed storage. Edna enjoyed visiting this congregation with her grandparents, Peter and Eva (Bartel) Schroeder.

The slow, hand-propelled ferry [top], used where the Vistula River flowed slowly, and the faster, steam-driven ferry [bottom], used where the Vistula flowed rapidly – the types of ferries Edna would have used before the War. After the War, MCC workers also used these services in their food and clothing distributions.

[Top:] *The gates to one of the Polish camps, guarded by the militia, similar to those that held Edna prisoner for three years from 1945 to 1948.*

[Bottom:] *For several months during the winter of 47-48, Edna, in her third prison camp, was ordered to work in the "Jewish Ghetto" of Warsaw (here, the photo of an unidentified barefoot woman), sorting bricks among the rubble.*

[Top:] *The Warsaw store where MCC worker Bob Fisher made his first contact with Edna, February 11, 1948, during a business trip to Warsaw. Edna, at the time, was taken daily from prison camp to work at this store, where she mixed butter, cleaned fish and chickens, and did other chores. The word "Lody" is the Polish word for ice-cream. At the time, this quickly reconstructed, temporary, make-shift store was still surrounded by bombed-out buildings. [Bottom:] Rolin, Pelplin, in northern Poland, the post-war MCC Center in Poland. A former estate, Rolin was comprised of a large two-story house with small, one-room brick houses nearby that had been home for the peasant workers.*

[Top:] *The MCC unit at Rolin, Pelplin, distributed food and clothing sent by Mennonites in Canada and the United States. Local Polish officials from the surrounding villages provided lists of those persons who were to receive help. Every MCC worker wore the MCC identifying insignia on a sleeve. It was also found on bags of flour, a main staple for distribution – in this case, originating in Menno Fast s home community of Goessel, Kansas.*

[Bottom:] *The "25 Men Tractor Unit," described by Rachel Fisher in her Introduction. The men spent a weekend at MCC Rolin, Pelplin, happy to get North American cooking for a change. Menno Fast was assistant director, and Fred Swartzendruber, director.*

[Bottom right:] *Two Mennonite sisters, Gundela [on left] and Helga Dyck, mentioned by Edna in her story. Their hands were sore from working in the fields for Polish people, pulling thistles without any gloves. MCC gave them gloves and other needed items.*

[Top:] *Rachel Fisher, Frau Bergmann, and Edna, at MCC Rolin, Pelplin, spring, 1948. Frau Bergmann gave the Fishers a painting she had found in an abandoned house which had belonged to some friends who had to flee the advancing Russian army. The painting, "The Gleaners," now hangs in the living room of Bob and Rachel Fisher's home.*

[Bottom:] *Edna and Rachel [center] with two Mennonite girls who had come for church and Sunday dinner (1948).*

Members of the MCC Unit at Rolin, Pelplin, in 1947: [Front row] Orval Shantz, Bob (Robert) Fisher, Rachel Fisher, Ruth Miller. [Back row] Menno Fast, Cliff Kenagy, Wilson Hunsberger (director), Emerson Miller.
When Edna left the unit in June, 1948, she notes in her story how the MCC workers each gave her their monthly allowance of $10 to help see her through, in her long walk from Poland to the West.

Edna, beginning her long walk to the West in June, 1948, in Szczecin. On her way to the train Edna saw a photographer taking pictures and selling them to pedestrians. Edna still owns this dress.

[Top:] The MCC Büro (Administration Building), Gronau, where Edna first went to fill out papers (September 1948). This "villa" is described below in the Documents section, "One Day in an MCC Camp."

[Bottom:] The MCC Krankenhaus (hospital), Gronau, where Edna underwent a medical examination soon after arrival, remaining there for a number of weeks until she gained strength.

[Top:] The camp's bread supply; [Bottom:] Unloading food at the Gronau camp.

[Top:] Food preparation at MCC Gronau: Buttering bread for the children. [Bottom:] One of the refugee "blanket rooms" Edna describes in her story: "They hung blankets from the ceiling to divide the large room into smaller rooms, and then they put beds in these 'rooms.' Sometimes there were two beds to a room, and sometimes four. It wasn t fancy, but at least we had our own space to sleep."

[Top:] *On the occasion of Edna's baptism in Gronau, June 12, 1949. Seated [from left]: The preacher from the Baptist Church, Siegfried Janzen, David Quapp (an MCC worker), and Cornelius Wall. Edna is among those standing, seventh from the right, just behind David Quapp.*

[Bottom:] *The Cunard White Star S.S. "Samaria," the ship which brought Edna to Canada in August 1949, one year after she first arrived at the MCC Camp Gronau.*

[Top:] Edna, with her Uncle Edmund and Aunt Lydia Schroeder, winter of 1950, outside their home in Saskatchewan. Edna is wearing the coat that Menno Fast had given her in Poland. Edna remembers, "It was a thick, heavy coat. It looked like fur, but it wasn t fur. I told Menno that it was too rich for me. I was just a poor girl, but Menno said that the winters in Saskatchewan were very cold, I would need a warm coat like that. I wore that coat for ten years." [Bottom:] Edna with her cousins, 1949, shortly after her arrival in Canada: Lydia Mandau, Erma Schroeder, Frieda Schroeder, Edna.

Edna, having just arrived in Saskatchewan, August 1949.

[Top:] On June 1, 1950, a double wedding! Henry and Edna [on the right], Henry's sister Annie and her husband Eugene [on the left].
[Bottom:] Edna, Henry (1954), with their oldest sons: Harvey, age three [in back]; and Bernie, age two [in front]. Edna is wearing the black dress made from the shawl that Rachel Fisher had given her in Poland.

[Top:] *Three of Edna's sons (1958), John, Bernie, Harvey [in front]; and Emma's younger son, Edmund, and Augusta Schroeder, Edna's mother. Edna's mother and Edmund emigrated to Canada in 1953. Emma had remarried a Polish man, and thus it took much longer for her to emigrate.*

[Bottom:] *Edna, Henry, and four of their five sons, ca. 1962: [left to right:] John, Bernie, David (in Henry's arms), and Harvey. In the background is Henry and Edna's first home, near Watrous, Saskatchewan. Gary was not yet born.*

[Top:] *Henry, Edna and five sons (1973). First full family portrait. [front:] Edna, Gary, David; [back:] Henry, Harvey, John and Bernie. Photo taken one week before Edna had a kidney removed.*
[Bottom:] *Thirtieth wedding anniversary, 1980 (Eugene and Annie on the left).*

[Top:] *Henry and Edna Thiessen (December 1995).*
[Bottom:] *Edna (1995), in the gray dress which she wore on her three months journey from Poland to MCC Camp Gronau in West Germany. Edna donned the dress for Rachel and Bob Fisher, who were visiting in the Thiessen home. The many holes in the dress have been neatly mended by Edna, and the dress continues to hang in her closet along with the black wool dress from Camp Gronau.*

[Top:] Henry and Edna Thiessen's home (1997), near Watrous, Saskatchewan. Since then, Henry and Edna have moved to a smaller place in Watrous, and their son David, and his wife Pat, now live on the farm.
[Bottom:] Bob and Rachel Fisher, with Edna and Henry (1995), in the Thiessen home on a Sunday, after returning from a worship service at the Philadelphia Mennonite Brethren Church.

Thiessen family photo (1998), taken soon after David and Pat's wedding. David and Gary are seated with Henry and Edna; Bernie, John and Harvey are in the back row. Besides the five daughters-in-law, as of September 1999 there were nine grandchildren and two great-grandchildren.

– Photographs suplied by: Menno Fast, Bob and Rachel Fisher, Jan Gleysteen, MCC Archives, Angela Showalter, Henry and Edna Schroeder Thiessen

IV

EDNA'S STORY,
THROUGH DOCUMENTS

Excerpted illustration, from Menno Fast's Occasional Journal, June 7, 1948:

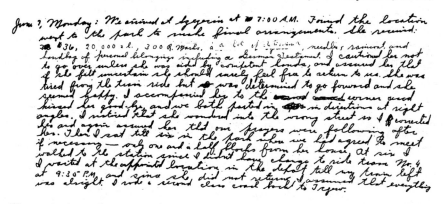

Transcription of excerpts from Menno Fast's journal, for June 5-8, 1948 (Edna also went by the nickname, Erna):

June 5, [1948], Saturday: Cliff went to Gdynia to get a raincoat for Erna. I tried to buy gas but couldn't get any for Sunday driving.

June 6, Sunday: The Fishers, Schwartzentrubers, Erna and I went to Ciminskis for Sunday services. On the way we visited the Wiehler sisters. We had planned to stop only a few minutes to take them along, but the landlord insisted that we have dinner with them, although it was only 9:30.... In the evening Erna and I took the train at 10:16. Alton and Joe relaxed. The Fishers planned to leave a couple of hours later.

June 7, Monday: We arrived at Szczecin at 7:00 a.m. Found the location, went to the park to make final arrangements. [Erna] received $36,* 20,000 zl[otys], 300 R[eichs] Marks, [several bars] of chocolate, needles, raincoat, and [a] handbag of personal belongings, including a German Testament. I cautioned her not to go over unless she was aided by competent hands, and assured her that if she felt uncertain she should surely feel free to return to us. She was tired from the train ride but was determined to go forward and she seemed happy. I accompanied her to the corner and kissed her good-bye, and we both parted in directions at right angles. I noticed that she wandered into the wrong street so I corrected her and again assured

(Edna received more dollars at the time of her departure, totaling $90.)

her that our prayers were following after her. Then I sat till six [o'clock] in the park where we had agreed to meet if necessary – only one and a half blocks from her house. At six [o'clock] I walked to the station since I didn't have change to ride tram No. 4. I waited at the appointed location in the depot till my train left at 9:35 p.m., and since she did not return, I assumed that everything was all right. I rode a second-class coach back to Tczew.

June 8, Tuesday: I arrived in Tczew at 6:50 a.m. Arrived at home just after the group had finished breakfast....

Edna's *Lebenslauf* (vita), December 7, 1948

Edna's hand-written "Lebenslauf," was written three months after her arrival in Gronau. In this short synopsis, Edna does not detail — and emotionally could not have detailed — her war-time experiences, nor her times in the prison camps. The date, November 1944, is many months too early. Only later, and then only very gradually, could Edna begin to sort out and interpret all her experiences, and line them up chronologically.

Translation: I, Edna Schroeder, was born on July 22, 1926, in Sezÿmin, Poland. My parents and I are Mennonites; we belonged to the Kazun Congregation near Warsaw, Poland. Until 1939 I attended the Polish elementary school in Sezÿmin. And until 1942 I attended the commercial school in Warsaw. After that I lived at home. In November 1944 we had to flee. While

fleeing, I became separated from my parents, and do not know to this day where they are. From 1945 to 1948 I worked in Warsaw as a domestic at the home of acquaintances. I have no relatives in Poland, only an uncle in Canada and one in the USA. I fear that, as a Mennonite, I could be forcibly returned to Poland, since I fled from Poland this year. I would like to emigrate from here to Canada, to my Uncle, who wants me to come.
– Edna Schroeder, MCC Camp Gronau, Gronau, December 7, 1948

"Ein Tag im M.C.C. Camp"

[Handwritten German:]

Ein Tag im M.C.C. Camp

Ein lauer Frühlingsmorgen liegt über einer kleinen westfälischen Stadt. Die ersten Sonnenstrahlen werfen einen freundlichen Schimmer über die kleinen Häuser und auch die Villa in der unsere Verwaltung untergebracht ist, wird in ein mattes, rotgoldenes Frühlicht getaucht.

Poetic description of MCC Gronau, in English translation:

"One Day in an MCC Camp"

A mild spring morning dawns over a small Westphalian city. The first rays of sunlight throw a friendly shimmer onto the small houses. The villa, in which our administration is housed, is also immersed in the subdued, golden-red light of morn.

Punctuality begins the pace of the day. The tired night watchman, having served through the long night, unlocks the gate to let in the office staff and cooks now arriving. The night nurses make their last rounds through the hospital rooms and women are already at work, washing down the house.

One of the first to appear is Miss [Irene] Bishop, the overseer of the kindergartens. Always smiling, she is first here, then quickly there, usually with her faithful companion, her small Volkswagen. Along with the trim, white troop of sisters led by the austere sister

Elise, the Director and his wife also soon appear. They too have indeed brought with them their quiet, friendly countenances from Canada.

Visitors come and go. The workmen are diligently at work, and the gardeners clear the last clippings from the walkways. In this manner the morning soon passes and the dinner bell sounds, reminding all to tend to their need of physical nourishment.

A hearty soup with potatoes, beans and meat is eaten with good appetite, followed by a short, cozy period of rest. Then in the afternoon the offices are again ardently buzzing. The women who were working in the kitchen in the morning are now sitting in the sun, sewing, darning and mending. Much longer lasts the afternoon, till at six o clock the bell rings for the evening meal, and we sit down to a meal of tasty groats.

Then the best part of the day is at hand: Preacher Janzen speaks. The room for worship is completely filled. Our cares and concerns of the day fall away, our faith is again strengthened, and our hope and trust in the help of the Lord brings inner joy, and quiets us. For this we thank Him from the depths of our souls.

Later the choir sings, or everyone gathers in front of the verandah to sing with guitar accompaniment, until Hausvater Löwen looks at his watch.

Then we each go to bed and hundreds of prayers ascend to heaven – our gratitude for another day granted us, intercession for our loved ones far away in the East.

May He grant sustaining strength for those working on our behalf, and for us, soon, a new homeland.

– Eugon Busse, Gronau, June 20, 1947

Excerpt from the November 4, 1949, report of Siegfried Janzen (Director of the MCC-Gronau office)to William Snyder, Akron, Penna., reaching back to the time Edna was there. Near the end of his report, Janzen notes, "when I returned to Gronau, I found it humming like a beehive":

William Snyder.......Akron, Pennsylvania   -5-

petrol if there had not been the good relationship Omar enjoys with the respective office officials. And again we would have never been able to have done the work in that short time had we not had ample supply of petrol. I still maintain that transportation is one of the most important factors to consider in our work.

The next point I want to mention is our accommodations. Needless to say our camp is well filled with 600 inmates. Still, I gave instructions to Omar and to his assistants in the camp to arrange for additional people coming in. If I remember correctly our camp strength stood at about 700. Soon after our telegrams had gone out to the various people living in the zones, and soon after our trucks had begun making tours, our camp strength began to climb steadily. I will not go into the details of explaining and describing the reshuffling and the re-arranging that was necessary. I remember one morning that the report on the camp strength was 1004. Two transports of some 70 people had come in from Berlin. There was a heavy strain on the kitchen. I will not say that everything could be arranged perfectly and that everybody was satisfied but I may and I will say that arrangements could be made to receive, accommodate and feed everyone who came in. How much I have wished that you people at home could have looked in during those days. Lists were being prepared in our office, documents were being sorted and got ready, the gestetner was kept busy for a good part of the time, telegrams and telephone calls were going out, trucks were milling around bringing in more people, food was being hauled, the Doctors were examining people and X-rays were being taken, our laboratory was working on Kahn tests, etc., the photographer was busy taking and developing passport photos. When the Labour officer, Mr. Tony Lamarre, came on Wednesday, we were able to present him our people.

Transcription: The next point I want to mention is our accommodations. Needless to say our camp is well filled with 600 inmates. Still, I gave instructions to Omar and to his assistants in the camp to arrange for additional people coming in. If I remember correctly our camp strength stood at about 700. Soon after our telegrams had gone out to the various people living in the zones, and soon after our trucks had begun making tours, our camp strength began to climb steadily. I will not go into the details of explaining and describing the reshuffling and the rearranging that was necessary. I remember one morning that the report on the camp strength was 1004. Two transports of some 70 people had come in from Berlin. There was a heavy strain on the kitchen. I will not say that everything could be arranged perfectly and that everybody was satisfied but I may and I will say that arrangements could be made to receive, accommodate and feed everyone who came in. How much I had wished that you people at home could have looked in during those days! Lists were being prepared in our office, documents were being sorted and got ready, the Gestetner [mimeograph machine] was kept busy for a good part of the time, telegrams and telephone calls were going out, trucks were milling around bringing in more people, food was being hauled, the doctors were examining people and X-rays were being taken, our laboratory was working on Kahn tests, etc., the photographer was busy taking and developing passport photos. When the Labour officer, Mr. Tony Lamarre, came on Wednesday, we were able to present [to] him our people.

Mennonitenflüchtlinge in den Westzonen

In his report to William Snyder, published above, Siegfried Janzen (Director of the MCC-Gronau office) mentioned that "the Gestetner was kept busy for a good part of the time." The document below is one such example of this printing productivity, entitled (in translation), "Mennonite Refugees in the West Zones [of Germany]: "Statistical Summary of the Gronau Central Files, April 1, 1948." Edna, not yet included in this listing, would join its ranks five months later. For the Polish Mennonites, the total was 366. Seventy had emigrated or died, leaving a total of 296. Of this total, 95 were males; 121, females; and 80, children.

Mennonitenflüchtlinge in den Westzonen

Bestand der Centralkartei Gronau
zum 1.4.1948

Gruppe	Gesamt-erfassung	Ausgeschieden durch Auswanderung, Tod usw.	(Bestand zum 1.4.1948
Russland-Mennoniten	11 657	4 458	7 2o5
Polen-Mennoniten	366	7o	296
Galizien-Mennoniten	263	6	257
Insgesamt	12 286	4 528	7 758

Aufteilung

Gruppe	Männer	Frauen	Kinder	Insgesamt
Russland-Mennoniten	2o81	3116	2187	7384 (72o5)
Polen-Mennoniten	95	121	8o	296
Galizien-Mennoniten	96	127	34	257
Insgesamt	2272	3364	23o1	7737 (7758)

Ausgewandert bezw. in Diepholz

Bestimmungs-land	Männer	Frauen	Kinder	Insgesamt
Paraguay	772	1312	1o83	3167
Canada	331	586	383	124o
andere Länder	4	9	2	15
Insgesamt	11o7	19o7	14o8	4422

Questionnaire which Edna filled out, March 26, 1949: Page One

Answers on page one show that Edna was Mennonite, had not been baptized. Her father was Mennonite, her Mother, Protestant (although we know from Edna's story that her Mother also attended the Mennonite church). Edna was willing to attend, weekly, Mennonite worship services, and stated that she was not attending non-Mennonite services at the time. She had attended Mennonite services up to 1939 in Kazun, Poland, and after September 1948 in Gronau. Edna was not a member of any other church group.

Edna's Questionnaire, March 26, 1949: Page Two

- 2 -

C. BERUFLICHES & GESUNDHEITLICHES

1. Wie viel Jahre Schulbildung haben Sie gehabt: *9* Wo:(Land) *Polen*
2. Erlernter Beruf: *keinen* Nebenberuf: *Landarbeiterin*
3. Hauptbeschäftigung vor 1940: *Schüler* Heutige Beschäftigung: *im Lager*
4. Wieviel verdienen Sie monatlich: ___
5. Wovon lebten Sie nach dem Zusammenbruch und vor der Währungsreform: *in Polen* *im Gefangenlager Warschau*
6. Sind Sie nach heutigen Verhältnissen mit Ihrer Wohnung zufrieden: *ja*
7. Sind Sie körperlich gesund: *ja* Wenn nicht, beschreiben Sie Ihr Leiden oder Gebrechen: ___
8. Sind Ihre Kinder unter 18 Jahre gesund:(nur für das Familienhaupt) ___
   Wenn nicht, beschreiben Sie Leiden: ___

D. AUSWANDERUNG

1. Möchten Sie um jeden Preis auswandern: *ja* Welches ist der Hauptgrund: *Bei meinen Angehörigen eine neue Heimat finden, ein christliches Leben fü* Andere Gründe: *Angst zum Russen*
2. In welches Land:(erste Wahl) *Canada* (2te Wahl) *U.S.A.*
3. Wenn nach Canada:
   a) Haben Sie einen Bürgen: *ja* Wie sind Sie mit ihm verwandt: *mein Onkel*
   b) Name und Adresse des Bürgen: *Edmund Schröder Drake Sask Bor 95 Canad.*
   c) Ihre Herausrufungsnummer ist: *34908*
   d) Sind Sie vor der I.R.O. Kommission gewesen: *ja* Wann: *16.11.48* Wo: *Gronau*
      Was war das Ergebnis: (Angenommen/Abgelehnt) *Pending*
   e) Falls schon vor canadischer Dienststelle erschienen, weshalb wurden Sie
      Abgesagt: ___ Wann: ___
      Zurückgestellt: ___ Wann: ___ Auf wie lange: ___
4. Wenn nach Süd-Amerika, in welches Land:(Paraguay/Uruguay) ___
   Wenn Grund Verwandtschaft ist, bitte Verwandtschaftsgrad angeben: ___
   Sonstige besondere Gründe:(Sprungbrett nach Canada,usw.) ___
5. Wenn nach U.S.A., aus welchen Gründen: *Möchte zu Verwandten*

will b. transport i cccr
(later Elizbth)

Page two notes that Edna had nine years of schooling in Poland, had no formal vocational training, had helped out with farm work, before 1940 had been in school, was currently working at the MCC Gronau camp, had previously spent time in a Warsaw prison camp, was satisfied with her present living environment, and was healthy. She wanted to emigrate, so as to find a new home in Canada or the USA with her relatives, and in order to lead a Christian life. She also had fears of needing to return to the Russians. Her Uncle Edmund Schroeder from Drake, Saskatchewan, was willing to be her guarantor. Her case was "pending," (this word in another handwriting).

Edna's Questionnaire, March 26, 1949: Page Three

- 3 -

E. VERSCHIEDENES

1. Sind Sie verheiratet/verwitwet: *nein* Mit wem — Name vor Heirat —

2. Sind Sie geschieden: *nein* In welchem Jahr: — Von wem —

3. Sind Sie standesamtlich und/oder kirchlich getraut: . *nein*

4. Haben Sie uneheliche Kinder *nein* Wieviel: — Name des Vaters —

5. Sind Sie verlobt: *nein* Ist Verlobte(r) Mennonit: — Reichsdeutsch:

6. Sind Sie bereit - wenn erforderlich - ohne ihn/sie auszuwandern: —

7. Ist Ihr(e) Mann/Frau verschollen: — Seit wann:

   Welche Nachricht haben Sie:

8. Waren Sie in der Wehrmacht: *nein* Wenn ja, von — bis —

   Waren Sie in der SS: *nein* Wenn ja, von — bis —

   Welche körperliche Spuren sind hinterblieben:

9. Waren Sie Mitglied der Kommunistischen Partei/Gottloser Bund? *nein*

   Waren Sie Mitglied der NSDAP oder einer ihrer Gliederungen: *nein*

   Wenn ja, Entnazifizierungsbescheid: Stufe I. II. III. IV. V. - nicht betroffen.

10. Wann kamen Sie nach Deutschland: *5.9.48.* Land der Herkunft: *Polen*

11. Staatsangehörigkeit vor 1939: *Polnische*

12. Wurden Sie in das Deutsche Reich eingebürgert: *nein* Wann: — Wo. —

    Erfolgte die Einbürgerung auf Wunsch oder auf Befehl: —

    Wenn auf Befehl, beschreiben Sie Einzelheiten: —

13. Wurden Sie in Polen angesiedelt: *nein, eigene Landwirtschaft*

14. Haben Sie Verwandte in russischer Verbannung: *nein* Wieviel: —

    Name und Adresse von Verwandten in Russland (Zwecks eventueller späterer MCC

    Arbeit in Russland:

15. Erhalten Sie Altersunterztützung, Witwen oder Waisenrente: *nein*

    Wenn ja, wieviel monatlich: —

16. Wenn erforderlich zur Bearbeitung, können Sie auf einige Tage ohne MCC Hilfe,

    nach Gronau kommen? *Bin im M.C.C. Lager Gronau*

zu 14 Frage: Vater von Polen verschleppt, Mutter ist noch in Polen.

Page three notes that Edna was not married, not a widow, not divorced. She
had no illegitimate children, was not engaged to be married. She had never
been in the Wehrmacht, or in the SS. She was not a member of the Communist
Party, or of the League of Atheists, or of the NSDAP. Edna came to Germany
from Poland on September 5, 1948, and was of Polish citizenship before
1939. She had not become a German citizen. She had not emigrated to
Poland, but was born there, where she, with her family, had their own farm.
She had no relatives who had been expelled by Russia, although her Father
had been "deported from Poland." Her Mother was still in Poland. Edna was
receiving no form of financial support.

Edna's Questionnaire, March 26, 1949: Page Four

- 4 -

17. Nennen Sie Verwandte, wenn auch noch so weitläufig, unter den Flüchtlingen
    in Deutschland (SEHR WICHTIG):

a) *Schröder Peter*   *11.12. 1907*   *Onkel*
    Name   Vorname   Geburtsdatum   Verwandtschaftsgrad
   M. C. C. Lager Epe
    Anschrift in Deutschland

b) _____
    Name   Vorname   Geburtsdatum   Verwandtschaftsgrad

    Anschrift in Deutschland

c) _____
    Name   Vorname   Geburtsdatum   Verwandtschaftsgrad

    Anschrift in Deutschland

d) _____
    Name   Vorname   Geburtsdatum   Verwandtschaftsgrad

    Anschrift in Deutschland

Vollständige Adresse:
Edna Schröder   Datum: *26. III 49*
(21a) Gronau / Westf
M. C. C. Lager (Clubhaus)   Unterschrift: *Edna Schröder*

───

                    N U R   F U E R   M C C

a) Reference Letter:

b) Personal Interview:

          ausgel. 4.8.49, Samaria" (34908)

Signature MCC Representative_____ Place of Interview_____Date_____

*Page four notes that Edna had an uncle, Peter Schroeder, born December 11,
1907, who was living in the MCC Camp Eppe. She gives her current Gronau
address, and the date, March 26, 1949, and completes the questionnaire
with her signature, Edna Schröder. MCC markings on page one, dated
February 4, 1949, show that Edna was slated for Canada. On page four is
also noted, in another hand: "sailed August 4, 1949, on the Samaria (#34908)"
(Edna s ID number).*

Edna's Request for Emigration to the USA

Edna also had relatives living in Philadelphia, Penna., which meant that the
USA also came into question as her new home. So, on May 18, 1949, she
applied to the Consulate of the USA in Bremen, asking to be accepted for
emigration to the USA (although Canada was her first choice).

Edna Schroeder   Gronau/Westf., den 18. Mai 1949.
                                  Enscheder Str. 24

An das
Konsulat der USA

B r e m e n
Haus des Reichs

Hiermit stelle ich den Antrag auf Aufnahme in die Warteliste
zur Auswanderung nach den USA und bitte um Uebersendung eines
Anmeldevordrucks. Ich bin am 22.7.1926 in Sezymin (Polen)
geboren.
Einen Freiumschlag mit meiner Anschrift fuege ich bei.

                                  Hochachtungsvoll!

1 Anlage.

Translation:

Edna Schroeder   Gronau/Westf., May 18, 1949
                              Enscheder Str. 24

To the Consulate of the USA, Bremen, Haus des Reichs

Herewith I am applying to be accepted into the waiting list for
emigration to the USA, and request that a registration form be
forwarded to me. I was born on July 22, 1926, in Sezÿmin, Poland.
Enclosed is a stamped, self-addressed envelope.

Respectfully, [Edna Schroeder]

[*Noted in pencil, in German, on the carbon copy kept in the MCC
Gronau office:* "Registration form filled out and sent in."]

MCC Gronau Director Siegfried Janzen's letter requesting action regarding the next step in processing Edna's emigration papers to Canada:

17 June 1949

CCCRR
34 DPACS Muehlenberg Camp
Hannover, BAOR 5

M/55 - SCHROEDER, Edna, Canadian Serial No. 34908

In confirmation of our telephone conversation
of a few days ago, I herewith request that the M/55
for the a/m person be transferred to IRO Fallingbostel where it will be processed.

Siegfried Janzen, Director
Gronau Unit

Excerpts from two MCC refugee lists, the first, showing her ultimate destination being with the Edm. Schroeders in Drake, Saskatchewan, and the second, the vessel on which she sailed, the SS Samaria, and the sailing date, August 4, 1949:

5040.	37269	Nickel	Anganetha	28. 7.92	Neuhorst	Housew.	Ar.Friesen,
5041.	37270	"	Franz	23. 1.31	Neuendorf	Farmh.	Steinbach,
							Box 590, Man.
5042.	32282	Rom	Helene	27. 4.24	Kronstal	Clerk	Friedr.Rom,
							18 Larch Toronto,Ont
5043.	34908	Schroeder	Edna	22. 7.26	Sezymin	Domestic	Edm.Schroe-
							der,Drake,
							Box 95,Sask

"	Lydia	18. 6.37	Wymyschle/Polen		TABINIA
"	Walter	29.11.40	"		
"	Paul	14. 5.42	"		
"	Hedwig	23. 7.43	"		
	Ziel: Jakob W. Matthies, 1186 Boundry Rd., Darrow, B.C.				
SCHROEDER	Edna	22.7.26	Dtsch.Sezymin	MCC-Lager Gronau	Canada 4.8.49 SS SAMARIA
	Ziel: Edmund Schroeder, Box 95, Drake, Sask.				
SCHROEDER	Erhard	22. 9.03	Nowosiadlo/Polen	MCC-Lager Gronau	Uruguay 7.10.48 VOLENDAM
"(Hammermeister)	Amalia	29. 4.09	Secynin/Polen		
"	Rudolf	23. 2.33	"		
"	Elfriede	9. 4.34	"		
"	Dieter	18.12.44	Troschin/Polen		

A letter of gratitude which Edna wrote in December, 1949, to the Janzens in Gronau:

Edna Schroeder

Liebe Geschwister Janzen.   ..., ... 14.12.49.

Box 95

Grüße Euch mit Psalm 116.

Zuerst wünsche ich Euch die schönste Gesundheit und den Segen des Herrn zu aller Euer Arbeit.

Es ist schon bald 8 Monate das ich bei meinem lieben Onkel weile. Es geht mir gut in Canade. Habe nicht⁺ zu klagen, sondern zu danken unserm Heiland für seine wunderbare Wege die Er auch an mir erwiesen hat.

Gerne denke ich auch an Gronau zurück, an die schönste Zeit meines Lebens. Bin unserm Herrn dankbar das ich auch hier bei seinen Kindern weilen kann. Habe schon so manche Segensstunde teilgenommen, und bin im Glauben gestärkt.

Wir haben auch noch immer gutes Wetter. Der Frost ist ziemlich hoch, aber ohne Schnee. Können noch jeden Sonntag zu Kirche fahren.

Vor par Tagen habe ich Post von meine liebe Mama erhalten. Bin froh das es Ihr auch gut geht in Gronau. Gerne möchte ich Sie auch bei mir haben. Leider kann Onkel nicht mehr Bürgen für Sie. Aber wir hoffen wenns Gottes Wille ist so fünd auch Mama noch ein Weg das Sie zu uns kommen kann. Die Bord sagte uns wie wir in Saskatoon waren das ich nach einem ½ Jahr für Mama Bürgen kann, wir wollen auch das beste versuchen.

Wir freuen uns über Onkel Peter Schroeder mit Fam. der am 17.12.49 hier an — kommen soll, und hoffen das es Ihnen auch hier gefallen wird. Wir werden dann eine schöne Familie sein (von 15 Personen)

Habe auch Frau Rosner mit Töchter besucht. Sie weilen nicht mehr hier, sind zu ihrem Onkel nach B.C. gefahren.

Will näher zum Schluß kommen mein Täubchen möchte auch gerne per Zeilen zu Ihnen schreiben

Ich danke Euch herzlich für alls gute. Möge es Euch der liebe Gott

A letter of gratitude, December 1949, to the Janzens in Gronau, continued:

alles vergelten, und viel Kraft schenken, das Euere Hände nicht müde machten werden, in dem großen Werk das Sie tuen.

Grüße Euch recht herzlich, und wünsche Gottes Segen zum Weihnachtsfeste, und viel Freude im neuem Jahr!

Der Herr sei Euere Hilfe und Stärke! Und sei Euer Trost!

In Christlicherliebe

Edna Schroeder

P. S.

Die herzlichste Grüße an Frl. Yake. Fam. Wall und Fam. Quapp.

Teure Geschwister im Herrn

Wir grüßen euch mit Jakobus 5 vers 7 und 8

Da unsere Liebe Edna an euch geschrieben fühlte ich mich gedrungen, auch ein paar Zeilen zu schreiben will euch in kurzen Worten dank sagen für all die Liebesarbeit die Ihr an unsre Lieben dort getan. Unsere Lieben Eltern Peter [illegible] sind ~~nun~~ nun schon anderthalb Jahre hier, sie lassen euch grüßen denken mit dank an euch zurück. Der Herr wird es euch lohnen, bleibet nur treu und unverzagt. Unser Flehen für euch ist daß der Herr euch viel Kraft schenken möchte nicht müde zu werden in der schweren Arbeit bis sie vollendet ist

Lieber Onkel Janzen Wir hätten noch eine Bitte an sie, Ob ihr dazu etwas tun könnt? Unsere Schwester Wanda [illegible] ist in der Russischen zone sie möchte gern nach Gronau her aber kein Geld sie soll 400 R. Mark, Oder 65 M. eure Geld haben sie bittet uns um Hilfe aber wir können nicht, könnt ihr sie helfen? wir könnten euch vielleicht zurück zahlen

[illegible]

A letter of gratitude which Edna wrote, December 14, 1949, to the Janzens in Gronau.
Translation (The words, "Edna Schroeder," and "Box 95," written at the top, and underlined, the markings of someone from MCC Gronau):

Drake, Sask., 14.12.49

Dear Brother and Sister [Siegfried and Margaret] Janzen,

I greet you with Psalm 116.

First of all I wish for you the best of health and the blessing of the Lord in all your work.

It is already almost four months that I have been here at my dear Uncle's place. I am doing well in Canada. I have nothing to complain about; on the contrary, I am thankful to our Savior for his wonderful paths which he has also rendered me.

I enjoy reminiscing about my time in Gronau, the loveliest period of my life. I am thankful to our Lord that I can also sojourn here among his children. I have already experienced many hours of blessing, and have been strengthened in my faith.

We are still having good weather. It is well below freezing, but no snow. We are able to drive to church each Sunday.

A few days ago I received mail from my dear Mother. I am glad that she is also doing well in Gronau. I would certainly also like to have her here with me. Unfortunately my Uncle can no longer be a guarantor for her. But we hope, if it is God's will, Mother will also find the way to come to us. The Board, last time we were in Saskatoon, said that in half a year I could be Mother's guarantor. We want to try for the best way.

We rejoice that Uncle Peter Schroeder and family are to arrive here on Dec. 17, 1949, and we hope they too will like it here. We then shall comprise a lovely family (of 15).

A letter of gratitude which Edna wrote, December 14, 1949, to the Janzens in Gronau.
Translation, continued:

I also visited Mrs. Rossner and her daughter. They are no longer living here, having moved to B.C. to be with their uncle.

I want to close since my little Aunt (Lydia) would also like to write you a few lines.

I thank you all from my heart for all the good you are doing. May our dear God compensate you for all this, granting you strength, that your hands will not tire in the great work that you are doing. Greet all the others cordially for me. I wish for you God's blessing during this Christmas season, and much joy in the new year!

May the Lord be your help and strength, and be your comfort!

In Christian love,

Edna Schroeder

P.S. My most cordial greetings to Miss Yake, Family Wall and Family Quapp.

Attached to Edna's letter of December 14, 1949, to the Janzens in Gronau, was a short letter written by her Aunt Lydia (Mrs. Edmund Schroeder): Translation:

Precious brother and sister in the Lord,

We greet you with James 5:7-8.

Since our dear Edna has written to you, I also felt compelled to write a few lines. I also want in short to thank you for all the works of love that you have shown to our loved ones. Our dear parents, Peter Guhrs, have been here already for a year and a half. They send their greetings and think back to you with gratitude. The Lord will grant recompense. Remain faithful and resolute. Our prayer for you is that the Lord may grant you much strength, that you do not tire in the difficult work, until it is completed.

Dear Uncle Janzen, we have one more request for you, wondering if you could do something. Our sister, Wanda Mandau is in the Russian Zone. She would like to come to Gronau, but has no money. She is asking us for help, but we cannot help her. Can you help her? We could then perhaps pay you back. We thank you for this in advance.

Please accept with love my poorly written letter. We wish you blessed Christmas festivities.

We greet you in thankful love, the Edmund Schroeders.

— *Documents: Menno Fast, MCC Archives*
— *Translations, Leonard Gross*

About Pandora Press

Pandora Press is a small, independently owned press dedicated to making available modestly priced books that deal with Anabaptist, Mennonite, and Believers Church topics, both historical and theological. We welcome comments from our readers.

Stuart Murray, *Biblical Interpretation in the Anabaptist Tradition*
(Kitchener: Pandora Press, 2000; co-published with Herald Press)
    Softcover, 310pp. ISBN 0-9685543-3-4
    $28.00 U.S./$32.00 Canadian. Postage: $4.00 U.S./$5.00 Can.
    [How Anabaptists read the Bible; considerations for today's church]

Apocalypticism and Millennialism, ed. by Loren L. Johns
(Kitchener: Pandora Press, 2000; co-published with Herald Press)
    Softcover, 419pp; Scripture and name indeces
    ISBN 0-9683462-9-4
    $37.50 U.S./$44.00 Canadian. Postage: $5.00 U.S./$6.00 Can.
    [A clear, careful, and balanced collection: pastoral and scholarly]

Later Writings by Pilgram Marpeck and his Circle. Volume 1: The Exposé, A Dialogue and Marpeck's Response to Caspar Schwenckfeld
Translated by Walter Klaassen, Werner Packull, and John Rempel
(Kitchener: Pandora Press, 1999; co-published with Herald Press)
    Softcover, 157pp. ISBN 0-9683462-6-X
    $20.00 U.S./$23.00 Canadian. Postage: $4.00 U.S./$5.00 Can.
    [Previously untranslated writings by Marpeck and his Circle]

John Driver, *Radical Faith. An Alternative History of the Christian Church,* edited by Carrie Snyder.
    (Kitchener: Pandora Press, 1999; co-published with Herald Press)
    Softcover, 334pp. ISBN 0-9683462-8-6
    $32.00 U.S./$35.00 Canadian. Postage: $5.00 U.S./$6.00 Can.
    [A history of the church as it is seldom told – from the margins]

C. Arnold Snyder, *From Anabaptist Seed. The Historical Core of Anabaptist-Related Identity*
(Kitchener: Pandora Press, 1999; co-published with Herald Press)
Softcover, 53pp.; discussion questions. ISBN 0-9685543-0-X
$5.00 U.S./$6.25 Canadian. Postage: $2.00 U.S./$2.50 Can.
[Ideal for group study, commissioned by Mennonite World Conf.]
Also available in Spanish translation: *De Semilla Anabautista*,
from Pandora Press only.

John D. Thiesen, *Mennonite and Nazi? Attitudes Among Mennonite Colonists in Latin America, 1933-1945.*
(Kitchener: Pandora Press, 1999; co-published with Herald Press)
Softcover, 330pp., 2 maps, 24 b/w illustrations, bibliography, index.
ISBN 0-9683462-5-1
$25.00 U.S./$28.00 Canadian. Postage: $4.00 U.S./$5.00 Can.
[Careful and objective study of an explosive topic]

Lifting the Veil, a translation of *Aus meinem Leben: Erinnerungen von J.H. Janzen*. Ed. by Leonard Friesen; trans. by Walter Klaassen
(Kitchener: Pandora Press, 1998; co-pub. with Herald Press).
Softcover, 128pp.; 4pp. of illustrations. ISBN 0-9683462-1-9
$12.50 U.S./$14.00 Canadian. Postage: $4.00 U.S. and Can.
[Memoir, confession, critical observation of Mennonite life in Russia]

Leonard Gross, *The Golden Years of the Hutterites*, rev. ed.
(Kitchener: Pandora Press, 1998; co-pub. with Herald Press).
Softcover, 280pp., index. ISBN 0-9683462-3-5
$22.00 U.S./$25.00 Canadian. Postage: $4.00 U.S./$5.00 Can.
[Classic study of early Hutterite movement, now available again]

The Believers Church: A Voluntary Church, ed. by William H. Brackney
(Kitchener: Pandora Press, 1998; co-published with Herald Press).
Softcover, viii, 237pp., index. ISBN 0-9683462-0-0
$25.00 U.S./$27.50 Canadian. Postage: $4.00 U.S./$5.00 Can.
[Papers read at the 12th Believers Church Conference, Hamilton, Ont.]

An Annotated Hutterite Bibliography, compiled by Maria H. Krisztinkovich, ed. by Peter C. Erb (Kitchener, Ont.: Pandora Press, 1998). (Ca. 2,700 entries) 312pp., cerlox bound, electronic, or both.
ISBN (paper) 0-9698762-8-9/(disk) 0-9698762-9-7
$15.00 each, U.S. and Canadian. Postage: $6.00 U.S. and Can.
[The most extensive bibliography on Hutterite literature available]

Jacobus ten Doornkaat Koolman, *Dirk Philips. Friend and Colleague of Menno Simons,* trans. W. E. Keeney, ed. C. A. Snyder (Kitchener: Pandora Press, 1998; co-pub. with Herald Press).
Softcover, xviii, 236pp., index. ISBN: 0-9698762-3-8
$23.50 U.S./$28.50 Canadian. Postage: $4.00 U.S./$5.00 Can.
[The definitive biography of Dirk Philips, now available in English]

Sarah Dyck, ed./tr., *The Silence Echoes: Memoirs of Trauma & Tears* (Kitchener: Pandora Press, 1997; co-published with Herald Press).
Softcover, xii, 236pp., 2 maps. ISBN: 0-9698762-7-0
$17.50 U.S./$19.50 Canadian. Postage: $4.00 U.S./$5.00 Can.
[First person accounts of life in the Soviet Union, trans. from German]

Wes Harrison, *Andreas Ehrenpreis and Hutterite Faith and Practice* (Kitchener: Pandora Press, 1997; co-published with Herald Press).
Softcover, xxiv, 274pp., 2 maps, index. ISBN 0-9698762-6-2
$26.50 U.S./$32.00 Canadian. Postage: $4.00 U.S./$5.00 Can.
[First biography of this important seventeenth century Hutterite leader]

C. Arnold Snyder, *Anabaptist History and Theology: Revised Student Edition* (Kitchener: Pandora Press, 1997; co-pub. Herald Press).
Softcover, xiv, 466pp., 7 maps, 28 illustrations, index, bibliography.
ISBN 0-9698762-5-4
$35.00 U.S./$38.00 Canadian. Postage: $5.00 U.S./$6.00 Can.
[Abridged, rewritten edition for undergraduates and the non-specialist]

Nancey Murphy, *Reconciling Theology and Science: A Radical Reformation Perspective* (Kitchener, Ont.: Pandora Press, 1997; co-pub. Herald Press).
Softcover, x, 103pp., index. ISBN 0-9698762-4-6
$14.50 U.S./$17.50 Canadian. Postage: $3.50 U.S./$4.00 Can.
[Exploration of the supposed conflict between Christianity and Science]

C. Arnold Snyder and Linda A. Huebert Hecht, eds, *Profiles of Anabaptist Women: Sixteenth Century Reforming Pioneers* (Waterloo, Ont.: Wilfrid Laurier University Press, 1996).
Softcover, xxii, 442pp. ISBN: 0-88920-277-X
$28.95 U.S. or Canadian. Postage: $5.00 U.S./$6.00 Can.
[Biographical sketches of more than 50 Anabaptist women; a first]

The Limits of Perfection: A Conversation with J. Lawrence Burkholder
2nd ed., with a new epilogue by J. Lawrence Burkholder, Rodney Sawatsky and Scott Holland, eds.
(Kitchener: Pandora Press, 1996).
Softcover, x, 154pp. ISBN 0-9698762-2-X
$10.00 U.S./$13.00 Canadian. Postage: $2.00 U.S./$3.00 Can.
[J.L. Burkholder on his life experiences; eight Mennonites respond]

C. Arnold Snyder, *Anabaptist History and Theology: An Introduction* (Kitchener: Pandora Press, 1995).   ISBN 0-9698762-0-3
Softcover, x, 434pp., 6 maps, 29 illustrations, index, bibliography.
$35.00 U.S./$38.00 Canadian. Postage: $5.00 U.S./$6.00 Can.
[Comprehensive survey; unabridged version, fully documented]

C. Arnold Snyder, *The Life and Thought of Michael Sattler*
(Scottdale: Herald Press, 1984).
Hardcover, viii, 260pp. ISBN 0-8361-1264-4
$10.00 U.S./$12.00 Canadian. Postage: $4.00 U.S./$5.00 Can.
[First full-length biography of this Anabaptist leader and martyr]

Pandora Press
51 Pandora Avenue N.
Kitchener, Ontario
Canada N2H 3C1
Tel./Fax: (519) 578-2381
E-mail: panpress@golden.net
Web site: www.pandorapress.com

Herald Press
616 Walnut Avenue
Scottdale, PA
U.S.A. 15683
Orders: (800) 245-7894
E-mail: hp%mph@mcimail.com
Web site: www.mph.lm.com